American Folk Dolls

Wendy Lavitt

American Folk Dolls

with photographs by Schecter Me Sun Lee

Alfred A. Knopf New York 1982

THIS IS A BORZOI BOOK PUBLISHED BY ALFRED A. KNOPF, INC.

Copyright © 1982 by Wendy Lavitt
All rights reserved under International and Pan-American Copyright Conventions.
Published in the United States by Alfred A. Knopf, Inc., New York,
and simultaneously in Canada by Random House of Canada Limited, Toronto.
Distributed by Random House, Inc., New York.

Photograph on page 12 courtesy of the Wachovia
Historical Society, Winston-Salem, N.C.

Library of Congress Cataloging in Publication Data
Lavitt, Wendy.
American folk dolls.
1. Dolls—United States—History—18th century.
2. Dolls—United States—History—19th century.
3. Folk art—United States. I. Title.
NK4894.U6L38   1982   745.592′21′0973   82-47839
ISBN 0-394-52024-6
ISBN 0-394-71132-7 (pbk.)

Manufactured in Japan
First Edition

FRONTISPIECE: *Little Girl with Rag Doll.* Anonymous, ca. 1825.
19th c. American portraits often showed children with their favorite
"boughten" toys or china dolls. This is a rare example of a little girl
holding a homemade doll. (Oil on canvas, 23½″ x 19½″) *Courtesy
of and photograph by the George E. Schoellkopf Gallery*

To Mel, Kathy, John, and Meredith
To my mother, Eve, and in memory
of my father, Ralph Adler

Framed paper doll from the Midwest.

Contents

Acknowledgments

Many people shared their valuable time and knowledge with me during the research and writing of *American Folk Dolls*. Their enthusiastic response to the project inspired me to seek another, and yet another, untold story of a homemade doll. I would like to thank the following museum staff members for their generous help:

Brenda Holland, Mary Jane Lenz, and Gary Galante, of the Museum of the American Indian, Heye Foundation, New York City; Mrs. Ruth Hagy, of the Chester County Historical Society, Pa.; Dinah Larsen, of the Museum of the University of Alaska, Fairbanks; Carolyn Weekley, of the Abby Aldrich Rockefeller Folk Art Center, Williamsburg, Va.; Linda LeMieux, of the Wachovia Historical Society, Winston-Salem, N.C.; Nancy Paine, of the Brooklyn Children's Museum; Ruth Green and Sylvia Sawin, of the Children's Museum, Boston; Ulysses Dietz, of the Newark Museum, N.J.; Mary Alice Kennedy, of the New-York Historical Society; Robert Bishop and Cordelia Rose, of the Museum of American Folk Art, New York City; Mrs. Lenon Hoyte, of Aunt Len's Doll and Toy Museum, New York City; John Noble, of the Museum of the City of New York; and Ann duMont, of the Memorial Hall Museum, Deerfield, Massachusetts.

I would also like to thank the following individuals: Corinne Burke, George Schoellkopf, Bernice Harvin, Cheryl and Robert Herman, Lola Redford, Nancy and Gary Stass, James Gentry, of the Southern Highland Handicraft Guild, Leslie Eisenberg, Alan Adler, Harvey Antiques, Elissa Cullman, William Ketchum, Loretta Holz, and Alan Winston.

A special word of thanks to Schecter Me Sun Lee, whose patience, skill, and enthusiasm were joyously transmitted to his photographs, and to Alice Quinn, my editor, whose encouragement and advice were invaluable. And to my partner, Margie Dyer, of Made in America, who was always there when I needed her.

In the same way as birds make a nest of anything,
children make a doll of no matter what.

VICTOR HUGO

Introduction

From the ancient dolls found at the sites of prehistoric Arctic villages, we know that handcrafted dolls were part of the North American scene long before the first European settlers ventured into the New World. English expeditions probably brought the first Old World dolls to this continent for trading with the Indians, who were fascinated with such trinkets. The explorers brought the famed "Bartholomew babies," inexpensive wooden dolls that were sold at the Bartholomew Fair and in the London streets. The first pictorial documentation of a doll in America was provided by artist John White, who in 1585 sketched a little Indian girl clutching both her mother and her newly acquired Elizabethan doll, dressed in proper English fashion. This formal wooden doll was far more elaborate than most children could ever hope to receive in the New World.

With shipboard space at a premium, children were forced to leave most of their toys behind. Occasionally, a doll's china head was smuggled on board, and probably a few dolls were made to ease the tedium during long voyages. According to Mrs. Sanford Meech, a descendant of the Brewster family, a wooden doll was fashioned for the Brewster children aboard the *Mayflower* by a Mary Chilton.[1] Few such early doll histories exist, since playthings were considered too unimportant to be recorded.

Once landed in America, children had little time for play—they were needed to help their families survive a hostile and unforgiving climate. Days of unending chores left few free hours and scant energy for making toys. Puritan ideology, which frowned upon frivolity and "amusements," warned children against the sins of idleness. But somehow

◄ Found in a New England shipyard town, this doll was probably made by a seafaring man in the mid-19th c. She is known as the "ship's prow doll," and is certainly the work of an experienced craftsman, who may have been a carver of figureheads. Wooden head, rag body, bisque hands that were perhaps borrowed from a china doll—a fine marriage of materials. The doll's dress is calico. Her legs and feet are made of cloth. Note her beautifully painted curls. (Height: 33″) *Courtesy of the Brooklyn Children's Museum*

dolls were born, in clandestine moments, from utilitarian objects. These dolls, fashioned with more love than expense, became part of American folk art. While made from whatever scraps were at hand, they possessed a unique beauty that shone through their simple appearance.

The shop ledger of a Salem, Massachusetts, general store included a farmer's purchases in 1651: "sugar for the goodwife and for the children a doll and a bird whistle."[2] Parents who lived far from town or could not afford the luxury of a "store" doll made do with homemade versions, as Mary Hall remembered from her pioneer childhood in Utah:

> We never had a "store" doll in our young lives. As a substitute we rolled some cloth about one or two feet long and fastened a three-cornered piece (a handkerchief), if we could find one, around the head. Later on when we could find a piece of white cloth, we would cut it out the shape of a doll and stuff it with wool, marking eyes, nose, and mouth, and sometimes making what looked like hair.[3]

In the more prosperous and peaceful times of the eighteenth century, the Puritan attitude toward toys and leisure relaxed as parents began to regard their children less as miniature adults and more as individuals with special needs of their own. Toys are mentioned in newspaper advertisements, letters, and inventories of the time.

Even Revolutionary War children owned dolls and other playthings, as attested by the excavation of a British campsite located at 204th Street, west of Broadway, in New York City. Toy pewter dishes, "buzzers," an earthenware lamb, and school slates were found, along with household articles.[4]

During the infamous Salem witch trials, homemade dolls—or "poppets," as they were then called—composed the main evidence against two eccentric old women. They

An exceptional example of a mid-19th c. cloth doll. The true fancy dolls of the day were china and wax ▶ dolls imported from Europe, but this is certainly a stylish doll. A real effort has been made to capture the fashion of the period, even to the full drop sleeves of her striped afternoon dress. (Note the leaf stitching on the linen pantalettes.) Her cap of human hair has been carefully plaited, and her velvet boots meticulously laced. In contrast to the daintiness of her waist, her hands are mere fists. (Height: 18") *Courtesy of Nancy and Gary Stass*

were tried and hanged for possessing dolls of "rags and hog bristles stuffed with goats' hair and other such ingredients" for evil purposes.

Many homemade dolls were silent eyewitnesses to history as they traveled across the Plains in covered wagons, broke through soldiers' lines in the Civil War, and pioneered remote Arctic regions. Often conceived in isolation and hardship, American folk dolls embodied triumphs of the spirit and the imagination. In frontier Utah, one mid-nineteenth-century mother wanted to surprise her daughters with wonderful Christmas presents:

> It was an impossibility to buy dolls, so she conceived the idea of making them each a rag doll. How this could be accomplished without their knowledge, she would have to work out after the children had retired. Each night she and her two older daughters would sew and work, work and sew until the task was finished; the result being two large rag dolls with shoes, stocking, chemise, panties, petticoats, and yellow dresses.
>
> The stockings were hung . . . and Christmas morning what should greet the eyes of the two little girls but the dollies hanging out of their stockings. When they took them to show Aunt Silver . . . she told them she would make them some faces. These turned out to be more caricatures than what the girls had expected. Poor Ruth was very unhappy and endeavored to wash hers with soap and water. . . . While trying to dry it out, she held it in front of the blazing fireplace and it was scorched. . . . Of course, through Mother's resourcefulness, the face was restored. There never were any dolls which had more care or fondling, more clothes made for them than these two dolls.[5]

The parents invested much time in these dolls, time devoted after long, hard days, but time that reaped treasured dividends of love. Children and parents gave a little bit of themselves to each doll, as Hannah Dalton recalled from her childhood on the Western frontier in the 1860s:

> Our playthings were very crude. . . . We would make our own dolls and some of them were quite nice. When mother could

spare a piece of cloth, she would cut a pattern the shape of the doll, and we would sew it up and fill it with sawdust, and then Mother would work eyes, nose, and mouth on it. But we were always happy and contented, and would dress them up as real dolls.[6]

During the Westward movement, children were forced to choose just one or two playthings to fit into already overcrowded covered wagons. Often, the one thing a little girl could not do without was a beloved doll. When she had more than one doll, the choice became excruciatingly difficult, as noted by Mabel Jones, whose father announced one day in turn-of-the-century Nebraska that they were moving westward:

At home one evening Mother told us to set out everything we wanted to take. We were down to the final stages of loading and, according to Mother, weight was the prime consideration. Brother Alma had to dump half his marbles, Lawrence had to pick a single favorite rock. When my turn came, Mother told me one doll was plenty.

The problem with taking one doll was that I had two, a china doll and a rag doll. I loved them equally well but the china doll had belonged to Mother. I took the rag doll with me out to play and gave it to Grace.

"Mom would never let me have it."

"Don't tell your mother. Hide my doll in the willows. Make a home for her and when you play, think of me way out West somewhere."[7]

If only the dolls themselves could speak!

Cloth Dolls

She was a beautiful doll. She had a face of white cloth with black button eyes. A black pencil had made her eyebrows, and her cheeks and mouth were red with the ink made from pokeberries. Her hair was black yarn that had been knit and raveled, so that it was curly. She had little flannel stockings and little black cloth gaiters for shoes, and her dress was pretty pink and blue calico.[1]

"Charlotte," the rag doll who brightened one Christmas for Laura Ingalls Wilder in the Wisconsin woods during the 1860s, typified the cloth dolls fashioned by countless pioneer mothers. Though rag dolls were made all over the world (the earliest being found in Egyptian tombs dating from 2000 B.C.), they are considered as American as patchwork quilts and corn pone. Sewn by pioneer women from scraps of materials, these dolls reflected the spirit of "making do." Rag dolls were often given as Christmas presents, and were fondly remembered by the recipients: "For Mary Alice there was a small doll, dressed in a wide skirt with white pantalettes gathered in about the ankles, as little girls wore them in the 1840s and the early 1850s. This had been made by Grandmother and Aunt Rebecca out of scraps and what else no one will ever know!"[2]

Most rag dolls were made of linen or unbleached cotton stuffed with bran, sawdust, or straw. Many mothers followed the advice in *The American Girl's Book* of 1831: "To make a large linen doll in the best manner, you will require, perhaps, a gallon of bran, which in the city will cost a few cents, in the country nothing."[3]

◄ This 19th c. cloth doll stuffed with bran was found in Utah. She was probably made by a child who had difficulty shaping and sewing the head, but her painterly skills made up for it. (Height: 14") *Author's collection*

A typical early rag doll's face was flat; its features were embroidered or painted on with fruit and vegetable dyes, and its hair was made from yarn, thread, animal fur, or even human hair. A carefully thought-out doll might have articulated fingers, but another might have mitten-like fists. The feet often turned in and were sometimes of uneven sizes. If seams had been sewn across the knees and elbows, the doll could bend and move about. The body reflected current styles, even to copying the popular wasp waist and ample hips of nineteenth-century ladies (see page 5).

When a doll grew worn, thrifty parents may have heeded a suggestion in *The American Girl's Book:* "When the face becomes soiled, it can be renewed again by sewing on a new piece of linen and painting it. . . ."[4] Laura Ingalls Wilder's beloved doll Charlotte received a new face after being left out in the rain: "Ma ripped off her torn hair and bits of her mouth and her remaining eye and her face. . . . Ma washed her thoroughly clean and starched and ironed her while Laura chose from the scrap bag a new, pale pink face for her and new button eyes."[5]

Some dolls were so altered by loving ministrations that any resemblance to their original appearance was purely accidental. "Polly," a doll belonging to a Quaker child in the first decade of the nineteenth century, underwent several "operations":

> At first Polly was a big rag baby of plain linen with black marks for nose, eyes, and mouth; then somebody cut her head off and replaced it with a plaster head which had bright rosy cheeks, dark eyes and curling hair. One day a friend offered to make her some new shoes and stockings, but said her feet were too clumsy to fit nicely; so poor Polly's legs were amputated just above the knees. When the new limbs were added and the new shoes and stockings put on, her arms and legs did not seem to match; so off they came, and new arms, with hands in little kid gloves, took their place. . . . She has had several heads in the course of her life, and her body has been covered once or twice. She used to always have a new dress for Yearly Meeting.[6]

In the days when little girls could sew a straight seam by age five, they naturally undertook many of their dolls' repairs themselves, and sometimes even made their own dolls. Big sisters, possessors of envied skills, were cajoled into mending worn doll clothing: "Almost every one of my sisters had some distinctive aptitude with her fingers . . . [one] had a knack at cutting and fitting her doll's clothing so perfectly that the wooden lady was always a typical specimen of the genteel doll world."[7]

Although fathers and brothers were more likely to whittle a wooden doll, a few attempted cloth dolls. Lacking the presence of a woman one Christmas in New England during the 1890s, Dan Tibbot was determined to make a rag doll:

> On the top of the tree, overlooking all this splendor, sat a rag
> baby Dan had made himself. It had a round flat head made out of
> a piece of Dan's shirt, and charcoal eyes and mouth. It had arms
> that stuck out like a pair of sore thumbs, and legs that crooked so
> many ways you couldn't count the turns. Over it all was a dress
> that Dan made out of a piece of white cloth.[8]

Many little girls yearned for store-bought dolls, and wealthy families ordered wax and china dolls from abroad. Even George Washington waited for an English shipment of dolls so he could obtain "a neat dress'd Wax Baby" for his stepdaughter. The families that could not afford such a fancy doll substituted the homemade rag doll in its place. Frontier children often recalled the efforts to substitute for manufactured toys at Christmas—"What toys we had were made by my parents. Mother made rag dolls, fried-cakes and honey candy dolls at Christmas time."[9]

As towns developed and parents grew more prosperous, china dolls and rag dolls with store-bought china heads found their way into Christmas stockings and were occasionally mentioned in a diary: "Our Christmases were not luxurious, but were events to always be remembered: a homemade doll and later a china one. . . ."[10]

Itinerant peddlers made room in their wagons for the popular china doll heads. Indeed, the day the peddler arrived was a grand event for both parents and children, for he relieved the monotony of frontier life and provided news and contact with the world they had left behind:

> It was always a gala day for us children when Peddler Marks
> came to town. He was a Jew, and he and his wife kept a little
> store at North San Juan which Mrs. Marks conducted in his
> absence. At first he carried his pack on his back, and as he became
> more prosperous he had a mule to carry it. Still later he rose to

the dignity of a horse and wagon. It was fun for us children to watch the unrolling of his goods from their big denim wrapper, and display on the floor of our sitting room calicos, woolens, and all sorts of "notions."[11]

General stores also carried china doll heads, and mail-order catalogues offered kid or china legs and arms as well. In the end, it was often left to Mother to create the doll out of these bits and pieces. Annie Kimball recalled:

My clever, thoughtful mother made the body of strong new Indian Head factory muslin and sewed on the beautiful china head. The body was large—the largest doll I had ever seen. Instead of stuffing it with sawdust or bran, patient hands had cut old soft cloth scraps which, as filling, made the body firm, yet soft. Seams at knees and elbows made flexible limbs which were sewed to the torso.[12]

European factories manufactured most china heads, but several American potteries also made them. These molds below were attributed to John Holland, a master potter in Salem, N.C., from 1821 to 1843. The ceramic doll heads were sold separately and attached later to cloth bodies.

Unique rag dolls were also made in Salem at that time. Dollmaking, like other arts, involved techniques passed along from one dollmaker to another. Elizabeth Chitty began making cloth dolls and soon taught her methods to her friends Maggie and Bessie Pfohl, who added their own touches. Maggie began the dolls in the 1890s, starting with an old German pattern of her mother's. She painted the heads with house paint, sanded them, then applied the features and hair with oil paints and varnished them (see page 19). The dolls had molded features, and carefully stitched fingers and toes, "and a backbone," she recalled. "You have to have a backbone. If you don't, they nod." The sisters made the dolls for fifty years, selling some and giving some away.[13]

Other popular materials for the heads of cloth dolls included tin and wax, but the wax heads were extremely perishable. If they did not melt from being left out in the sun or placed too close to the fire, they often met other unkind fates:

> Velma Sankey had a sawdust-stuffed doll with a wax head. The cheeks were rouged and the eyes painted. Velma took very good care of her doll by wrapping the doll's head in cotton when she put it away after play. One day she came home from school to find one of her brothers had taken a bite out of the tinted paraffin cheek of the treasured doll.[14]

Many children played with topsy-turvy or double-ender rag dolls that delightfully presented two dolls in one. With a head on each end of a single body, sometimes concealed by a long skirt, the topsy-turvy doll often took its characters from fairy tales and nursery rhymes. Little Red Ridinghood and Grandmother or the Wolf were a favorite combination. Many double-enders were Black and white dolls originating in the South, although children throughout the country played with them (see pages 22 and 23). The early topsy-turvy dolls were rooted in folklore, such as the Pennsylvania hex doll with both human and pig heads now residing peacefully in the Mary Merritt Doll Museum, Douglassville, Pa. In the eighteenth century, the hex doll was used for casting spells and curing warts.

Dolls belonging to Amish children form a special group, mirroring the customs and beliefs of the Amish people. Calicoes and other printed material were thought too worldly, and thus Amish parents dressed their children's dolls in the same plain clothes the children wore. Dolls remained faceless, following the commandment in Deuteronomy 5:8:

> Thou shalt not make thee any graven image, or any likeness of any thing that is in heaven above, or that is in the earth beneath. . . .

Once in a while, a child could not resist adding eyes, nose, and mouth to a favorite doll, usually in pencil, which could be easily removed if necessary. Mrs. Raymond Burkholder, of Napanee, Indiana, remembered that she originally made a doll without a face, but one was later added at her grandchildren's request. This was the exception rather than the rule. To this day, facelessness remains the outstanding characteristic of Amish dolls. "Swartzentruber" dolls, made in the strictest Amish sects, were even more basic, not only faceless but made without arms or legs, harking back to the dolls of primitive people.

Cloth dolls have their own celebrities, who enjoyed connections with famous people or events. Known as "Association dolls," these figures make history come alive. The oldest Association doll, "Molly Brinkerhoff," now minus one arm, has seen better times since her youth in pre–Revolutionary War days on Long Island. In 1776, oncoming British soldiers caused the Brinkerhoff family to flee their home, first burying their prized possessions (including Molly) in a trunk in their backyard. After the war, Molly was unearthed and loved by successive generations of Brinkerhoff children. Although her linen body is covered with repairs and her clothes all long since missing, Molly still greets an occasional visitor to her Vermont home where she lives with a Brinkerhoff descendant. A small plaque, made when Molly was exhibited at a fair about the time of the Civil War, reads:

MOLLY BRINKERHOFF

I am not made of dust or wax
But homespun linen stuffed with flax.
No human being treads the earth—
That was alive at Molly's birth,
Many score years have I, old Molly,
Kept the Brinkerhoff children jolly.

During the war of '76—
The clothes I wore were in a fix—
In oaken chest deep in sand—
I was buried on Long Island strand
There safe from British and Tories I lay
Till the last of the Redcoats skedaddled away.

Presidents and their wives have inspired dolls, including homemade rag dolls. George and Martha Washington prompted an enormous group of objects made in their likeness, from reverse glass paintings to portrait china and dolls of paper, wood, and cloth (see page 26).

During the tenure of John Quincy Adams, a doll named Sally, belonging to his grandchildren, won fame as "the White House doll." She is a large cloth doll with a painted face and she wears a cheery dress of red and white calico. Handed down through the Adams family, she lives with Miss Mary Louise Adams Clement, who says: "Sally is still very much of a personage, although now she leads a quiet life in Virginia and rarely makes public appearances, except at an occasional exhibition."[15]

Many dolls were first made for family and friends, and then turned into commercial ventures, as was so of the famous Izannah Walker rag doll, the first cloth doll to be patented, in 1873 (see page 32). Izannah Walker lived and worked in Central Falls, Rhode Island. Her niece described her aunt's efforts in a letter to the Providence *Bulletin:*

> Family tradition tells of her struggle to perfect her work and of the long wrestling with one problem, how to obtain a resistant surface to the stockinette heads, arms, and legs, without cracking or peeling. With this problem on her mind, Aunt Izannah suddenly sat up in bed one night to hear a voice say "use paste." It worked. . . . Aunt Izannah always deplored the fact that she was not a man. However, she made dolls and doll furniture, tinkered with household gadgets, designed a parlor heater "that beat Ben Franklin's," raised canaries, dabbled in real estate, and was looked upon with admiration by male contemporaries because of her skill with carpenters' tools, so perhaps she was resigned. She used her own handpress and dies for the shaping of her dolls' heads and bodies; all of the little hands and feet were hand-sewn.[16]

Whether or not a cloth doll achieved the technical sophistication of an Izannah Walker doll, the fame of an Association doll, or remained anonymous, it was loved and treasured beyond its worth by children who instinctively understood its true value. Perhaps *Harper's Bazaar* best expressed this phenomenon: "Even to the small girl, who cannot understand why or argue it out, there is a flavor of old-time charm about a good rag doll that the finest miniature lady or baby from Paris does not possess."[17]

One little girl, Lucy Larcom, admitted that her rag dolls were "limbless and destitute of features, except as now and then one of my older sisters would, upon my earnest petition, outline a face for one of them, with pen and ink. I loved them, nevertheless, far better than I did the London doll that lay in waxen state in an upper drawer at home—the fine lady that did not wish to be played with, but only to be looked at and admired."[18]

Rag dolls, primarily intended for children, appealed to adults as well, with many a grown-up treasuring a favorite doll. In 1915, Johnny Gruelle was searching through his mother's attic and found an old rag doll she had played with as a child. Its lovable, though dilapidated, condition inspired him to write a story about a doll he named Raggedy Ann. The rest is history: out of his story was born a rag doll beloved by millions of adults and children (see page 18).

Even a Union soldier fell prey to the charm of a rag doll found on a Southern plantation. Keeping it as a talisman, he carried it throughout the war until he returned safely home (see facing page). Confided in and hugged, wept over and tenderly cared for, rag dolls have received more love than any other type of doll. They have, indeed, seen many children "safely home." The doll Minnie Brown embraced one Christmas in the 1870s stands for the love behind all rag dolls:

> It was a pretty doll, about twelve inches high. The body was made of cream-colored factory cloth, and it was stuffed with wool. It had a pretty shaped head and arms and legs. Its hair was made of fine gray yarn, which had been unraveled from a child's sweater. The yarn was very curly. My mother was well trained in hand-sewing, and the face of my doll was a piece of art; the eyes, nose, and mouth, were perfect in shape. My doll was completely dressed. Its underwear was made of white material. The panties were trimmed with homemade lace and came down to its ankles in length. The little white chemise was also trimmed with lace. The pretty petticoat was tucked and lace adorned its edges. The pink calico dress and bonnet to match made this doll the most beautiful doll in the world. . . .[19]

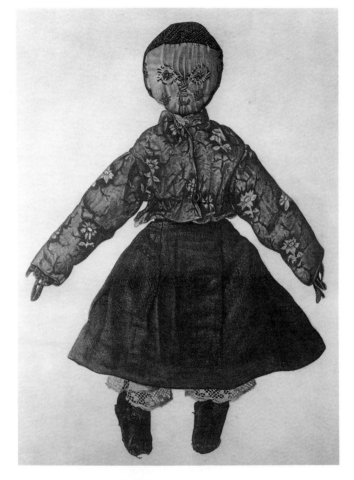

A painting, by Irwin Stenzel, of a Southern Civil War doll, executed as part of a WPA project. Her hair is made of wool suiting material, and her blouse of chintz fabric. Note the lace pantalettes and the intricate stitching of her cheeks. *Courtesy of and photograph by the National Gallery of Art, Washington Index of American Design*

The Elizabeth Chitty (left) and Maggie Bessie dolls from Salem in the 1890s, described on pages 12–13. (Height: left, 30″; right, 13½″) *Chitty doll: courtesy of and photograph by the Wachovia Historical Society, Winston-Salem, N.C. Maggie Bessie doll: courtesy of and photograph by Old Salem, Inc., Winston-Salem, N.C.*

◄ The first Raggedy Ann doll for sale, made in 1918. Her hair is of brown yarn and she has a celluloid heart tucked inside her chest, added after angry parents who bought dolls from the first (recalled) batch complained she did not have the famous heart. This particular doll recently flew to Indianapolis, hometown of Johnny Gruelle, author of the celebrated Raggedy Ann and Andy books, to receive the key to the city she is proudly displaying on her apron strap. (Height: 16″) *Courtesy of and photograph by the Museum of the City of New York*

These turn-of-the-century rag dolls (known affectionately by their owners as "the Funk family") were found in Pennsylvania. They were probably made and dressed by children who raided the attic for trimmings, and were certainly conceived as a family or a group of friends. Their lumpy heads are covered with muslin; their thread hair refuses to be combed. But the style of their clothes—the gold silk finishing touches, the cast-off brooches and cutout dress ornaments, the silver trimming, the lace on the calico dress—is in the spirit of children "dressing up." Faces were drawn on the cloth heads and the clothes were carefully sewn. The doll in the calico print, once a composition doll, retained her original arms and legs; by sewing a cloth head over what must have been a broken head, the dollmaker made her a member of the group. (Height: 15"–23") *Courtesy of Nancy and Gary Stass*

The simplest cloth doll of all. A 19th c. homespun linen-wrapped doll made by someone who did not have the time or materials (or perhaps the patience) to stuff and sew a proper cloth doll. She is very small and has faded with time, her once blue dress now a mottled tan. (Height: 5") *Author's collection* ►

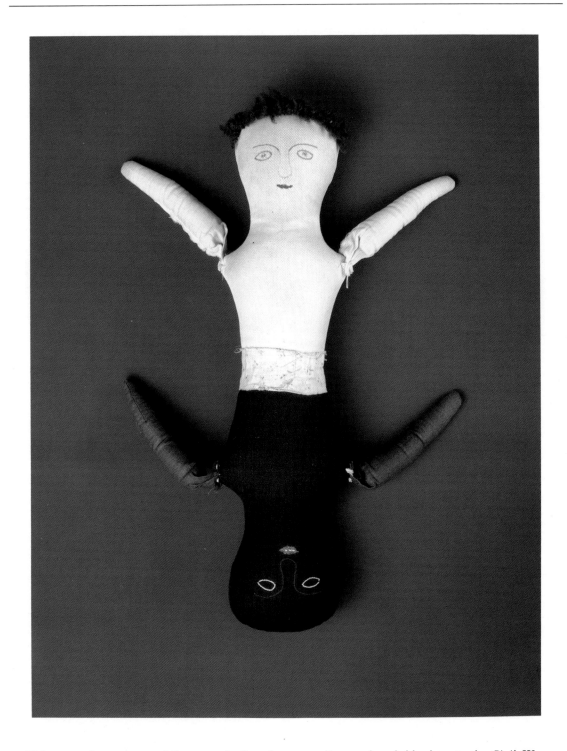

This unusual topsy-turvy doll was made from homespun linen and probably dates to the Civil War Perhaps topsy-turvy dolls grew out of the Pennsylvania hex dolls, but it's more likely that they originated in plantation nurseries. It has recently been suggested that these dolls were often made for Black children who desired a forbidden white doll (a baby like the ones their mothers cared for); they would flip the doll to the black side when an overseer passed them at play. Note that there are no irises in the Black doll's

eyes, but the teeth are carefully defined. Did the maker run out of black cloth for the arms or did she choose brown cloth because she liked it? (Height: 11″) *Courtesy of Bernice Harvin and Kelter-Malcé*

Another version (above)—this one late 19th c.—of the topsy-turvy doll, with painted features. Note that the heads are turned in opposite directions. (Height: 15″) *Author's collection*

Two sisters whose faces were obviously painted by the same hand, ca. 1870. They are true New England country dolls, cousins to the Utah doll on page 8. One has fur hair and leather hands and feet, the other wool hair and muslin hands and feet. (Height: each, 18″) *Author's collection*

This group of 19th c. cloth dolls, with quaint hats and skillfully embroidered faces, rests against a miniature Hoosier cabinet. They are dressed in homespun and calico and are almost certainly Southern dolls. (Height: 10″–20″) *Courtesy of Bernice Harvin and the author*

An early 20th c. George and Martha Washington pair with oilcloth faces and cotton bodies. (Height: left, 25″; right, 24″) *Courtesy of and photograph by the Chester County Historical Society*

A full spectrum of Amish dolls, from the rare boy dolls—one with a cap (front row, third from left), the ▶ other dressed in faded denim work clothes (front row, far left)—to the customary Amish ladies in their black bonnets. The dolls with the dark faces were made by members of especially strict Amish sects that allowed only blue or gray faces. (Making a likeness was considered sinful, but sometimes a child couldn't resist and penciled a face!) These dolls, though made in the early part of this century, respect deeply rooted traditions by wearing exact copies of the plain clothing that Amish children and adults have always worn. (Height: 6″–16″) *Courtesy of* Made in America

This stern-faced matron of the late 19th c. must have ruled the other dolls in the nursery with an iron hand. Her hair and features have been painted on her oilcloth face, and her no-nonsense dress is of red and white polka-dot cotton. (Height: 21″) *Courtesy of and photograph by the Chester County Historical Society*

An exceptional example of a cloth doll from New York State, made in the late 19th c. Her blue eyes are ▶ painstakingly embroidered, as are all her features, including each strand of her hair. (Note the delicate leaf stitching of the eyebrows.) She is holding a homemade cat typical of the toys of the period, and her dress is a calico print. Garters hold up her cotton stockings. Exceptional care has been lavished on her hands—and the ring that adorns the middle finger of her right hand is attached by a little string to her dress so she won't lose it! (Height: 30″) *Courtesy of Nancy and Gary Stass*

This 19th c. Southern gentleman, with his top hat and cape, white satin vest, and patent-leather pumps, is ready for an evening's divertissement. His head is made of kid, with painted features, and his hair is of yellow yarn. (Height: 13") *Courtesy of and photograph by the Shelburne Museum, Shelburne, Vt.*

Perhaps the most startling thing about this otherwise "proper" 19th c. cloth lady are her rouged cheeks. While her cape is of elegant silk and velvet, her dress is a plain cotton polka-dot print. (Height: 17½") *Courtesy of and photograph by The New-York Historical Society*

◄ This stately New England doll—unusually refined for a cloth doll—is wearing a paisley morning dress of the 1870s. (Height: 8") *Courtesy of Nancy and Gary Stass*

This lady is resplendent in a matching blue and white muslin print bonnet and dress. She is stuffed with homespun cloth; her features are inked; the hair in her pigtails is real. She belonged to the family of Joshua Wilder, a clockmaker of note in Hingham, Mass., in the 19th c. (Height: 16″) *Courtesy of and photograph by the Shelburne Museum, Shelburne, Vt.*

◄ Two striking examples of Izannah Walker's popular cloth dolls, made in Rhode Island and patented in 1873. Miss Walker probably turned out more than a thousand dolls—each with a characteristically childlike demeanor. They were made of successive layers of cloth and paste, then painted with oils. (Height: each, 15″) *Courtesy of and photograph by the Museum of the City of New York*

Corn Dolls

For the early settlers of America, life revolved around corn. Corn and its products became the staples of pioneer life. Without it, the colonists would have starved. Mattresses were filled with cornhusks. Entire meals consisted of corn soup, corn bread, pudding, and fried cakes. Popcorn-decorated trees, corn-mash whiskey, and toys fashioned from discarded corncobs enlivened many a frontier Christmas.

While farmers in Europe had grown corn for centuries, they relied on the wind for seed distribution. The settlers in the New World quickly noted the more efficient methods of the Indians, who carefully sowed and fertilized their crops. The making of corn dolls became a delightful by-product of the colonists' corn economy. Corn figures were not new to the English immigrants, as they had long been featured in harvest celebrations in England.

Despite the popularity of corn dolls, very few early examples survived. Far from being handed down from generation to generation, they were simply swept into the dustbin or destroyed in play. Small animals found their sweet kernels tasty and little children easily tore them apart. The earliest corn doll was found in an undisturbed seventeenth-century dwelling in Cutchogue, Long Island, in 1940. Amid many household articles were "three old homemade dolls of twigs bound together and wrapped with hand-woven linen—and one with a corncob head."[1]

There were two types of corn doll: cornhusk and corncob. Some dolls were combinations of both. The first step in making a husk doll required the careful removal of the cob from the husks. After the husks were soaked in water until pliable, they were often colored with fruit and vegetable dyes. Further steps in making a cornhusk doll are

◄ In her cotton plaid pioneer dress, this Mohican cornhusk doll with her will-o'-the-wisp hair comes from Stockbridge, Wisconsin, and reflects a blending of the Indian and pioneer cultures. (Height: 10″) *Courtesy of the Museum of the American Indian, Heye Foundation*

described by May Ritchie Deschamps, a dollmaker in Swannanoa, North Carolina: "The shucks must be worked damp," she says, "and you save the cleanest ones for the dress; sometimes I dye those. . . . First I roll the hands; then make the head. The body is made in two pieces."[2] The corncob doll was the simpler of the two types, and could be made by sculpting the head and body from a single cob, or by pulling the husks over the cob to make the head. Arms could be braided husks.

As Americans moved westward, children continued playing with these dolls, occasionally mentioning them in oral histories, diaries, or letters. In southwest Virginia, Lizzie Steele remembers Christmas in the mid-nineteenth century: "At times there were puzzles or whistles for the boys which had been whittled out of wood by my father or perhaps a cornshuck doll or some other pretty for each of us girls."[3] Generations of women fondly recalled transforming these simple dolls into elaborately dressed ladies, using corn-silk for their hair and dried sunflowers for their hats, which were then trimmed with chicken feathers.

The cornhusk doll allowed for more detailing than a plain corncob doll, and many varieties were created by the children and their parents. Jane Adams recalled how she and her friends made these wisps of dolls, starting in July when the first ears of corn rose in the field:

> About half an hour before supper we'd go into the garden, pick a dozen good fat ears of corn, shuck them, and pop them in the boiling water. I'd make a little wad or ball for the head, place it in the center of the leaves, and fold them over in half, tying the husks just under the head. Then I'd twist two leaves together to make the arms, tying them at the wrist. . . . If I was making a woman I trimmed the leaves to make a skirt, maybe taking some berries to color it, making a shawl from the bottom edge of the tougher outer leaves. . . . If I was making a man, I cut the leaves and tied them at the knees and ankles.
>
> In the late summer when the fields with corn were getting ripe I would make whole families: the parents out of the larger field corn, the children out of the sweet corn. They could have brown or yellow hair, depending on whether I used the old silk

A WPA drawing by Wilbur M. Rice. The intricate braiding of the husks, particularly of the horse, achieves an effect kindred to that of fine basketry. *Courtesy of and photograph by the National Gallery of Art, Washington Index of American Design*

or silk from the youngest ears. This was glued on or tied in with the head braided, cut short, curled if I used the old silk, or left hang long. I'd take a fine paintbrush or feather or twig and use berry juice for the faces, maybe gather bits of wool from the sheep and mat it into bits of clothing. . . . When acorns started getting ripe I would sometimes enclose one of them as the head, leaving the brown face out with the corn leaves around it. Some of the dolls had twigs or pipe cleaners for arms and legs, or I would put a wire in the center of each limb to shape them."[4]

For little boys, cornhusk dolls were made with accompanying horses, as illustrated by the Index of American Design drawing on page 37. Henry Dupont, growing up in the 1860s, recalled loving his homemade doll with its cornhusk head and rag body far more than any of his store-bought toys. Sometimes the body of a doll would be made from cornhusks and the head fashioned from another material. Paul Engle described Christmases in Iowa at the turn of the century: "And there would usually be a cornhusk doll, perhaps with a prune or walnut for a face, and a gay dress of an old corset-cover scrap with ribbons still bright."[5]

Some very elaborate cornhusk dolls made in the late nineteenth century, with husks meticulously shaped into beribboned, flowered bonnets accompanied by parasols and purses, suggest the work of seamstresses who costumed the fashionable ladies of the time. The doll pictured on page 42 is on view at the Essex Museum, Salem, Massachusetts, along with other cornhusk ladies who have been seen in duplicate versions in various parts of the United States. It has been suggested that these dolls might have served as milliners' models that found their way into the arms of lucky little girls whose mothers had purchased expensive hats.

Corn dolls still remain a popular form of folk art in Southern mountain regions, flourishing in cottage industries and craft guilds, echoing the days when corn was king. Isadora Williams, a crafts teacher in Knoxville, Tennessee, during the 1930s, recalled her early days with the "women who do things with their hands":

I came here in '31 to organize a curb market. No, not crafts. Vegetables, fruits, baked goods. But before I'd been here a year they asked me to work with the women who "do things with their hands." . . . I took it with some misgivings, and it has led to the most rewarding work I could have possibly done. You see, the women had to teach *me*. I sat down at the feet of these old ladies and learned. One day there was an order for a shuck doll. I'd never heard of one. At every meeting I went to, I asked. Finally a Mrs. Rogers up in Hawkins County said, "When I was a little girl, my grandmother made me a shuck doll and I believe I can make it." Next time I went back, she'd made four, all different. We gave them names, and named one "Molly," after her. The other three didn't sell at all, but "Molly" is still selling. In one year she went to twenty-three states and three foreign countries.[6]

In *Handicrafts of the Southern Highlands*, one of the first books to explore the craft traditions of the mountain people, Allen Eaton described various cornhusk dolls and dollmakers. While Mrs. Mollie Rogers, of Mooresburg, Tennessee, made doll families with corn-silk hair and painted faces, another Tennessee woman fashioned groups of dolls engaged in the everyday tasks of churning butter, milking cows, and driving sheep. And in Virginia, Mrs. Marshall Count's dolls portrayed mountain people, elves, clowns, animals, and crèche figures.[7]

In making their dolls, women stole precious hours from chore-filled days to painstakingly work the husks into the required shapes. The results provided great satisfaction, as an Arkansas dollmaker expressed in a letter to Carl Fox, author of *The Doll*:

I have made dolls for about thirty-three years, raised our children, keeping house, making a garden, raising chickens, milking cows, raising rabbits, canning vegetables and fruits and berries. . . . I made and sold dolls. Made them mostly at night. . . . I don't think anyone else makes the dolls like I do for I just studied these dolls and how to make them myself. . . . All of my cornshuck dolls are characters of people I can remember when I was five years old, from 1906 on up through my childhood.[8]

A group of cornhusk dolls, made in the 1930s, in brightly colored costumes with corn-silk hair. Note the accordion player's Lord Fauntleroy outfit. All four are the work of the same dollmaker. (Height: each, 5″) *Courtesy of and photograph by the Chester County Historical Society*

◄ A 19th c. cornhusk doll made by a Seneca Indian. Her black moiré hair is braided and tied with a red ribbon. She wears a purple tunic with silver tokens and a red kerchief, and her underskirt is decorated with blue and white beadwork. She probably belonged to a Christian Indian servant, because she was found in the estate of Bishop Wilson, a missionary in the Great Lakes area. (Height: 10″) *Courtesy of and photograph by the Abby Aldrich Rockefeller Folk Art Center, Williamsburg, Va.*

Two cornhusk dolls that show a range of styles, from simple to elaborate. The tall lady, with her parasol, purse, and bonnet complete with flower, might have been made by a milliner in the 1890s as a giveaway. The small doll beside her is hard to date. She is made from husks dyed brown; her features are inked on. Her green cornhusk dress is also dyed. (Height: 4″ and 12″) *Author's collection*

A pair of Southern cornshuck dolls, painted and varnished to the nines, made in the early 20th c. to be ▶ sold as "tourist dolls." Even the plaid apron is made of cornhusks. (Height: left, 9″; right, 11″) *Courtesy of Aunt Len's Doll and Toy Museum*

Wooden Dolls

> I have a very ugly wooden doll with clever joints, which was whittled by my great-great-grandfather about 1790. It warms my heart when I look at it and think of my great-grandmother as a little girl, wanting to possess a doll and having a father who understood and tried to fulfill the need. What time and patience it must have taken with crude tools and poor light.[1]

Early wooden dolls like the one belonging to Edith Standforth's great-grandmother were carved from the sturdy trees of the frontier that provided all the necessary wood for home and industry. At the end of the day, after stacking piles of logs, men and boys relaxed by whittling toys and whimseys with prized jackknives. The wood was all around them, and in true pioneer tradition they created gifts for their loved ones out of leftover scraps of wood. When cloth could not be spared for a rag doll, wood from a tree stump or even a worn-out household object could be turned into a doll. Potato-masher dolls lined with cracks telling of their years of smashing lumps out of boiled potatoes, spoon dolls that once stirred soups, and clothespin dolls wrapped in calico skirts graced frontier kitchens before their transformations. In Utah, a frontier child's Christmas was brightened by a clothespin doll in the mid-nineteenth century: "Mamie had taken a long clothespin from her mother's peg sack and had spent hours in hemming, folding, dyeing, tying, painting, and padding a doll for Clara. . . ."[2] When a bed gave out, a lucky child might receive a bedpost doll (see facing page), the head carved by her father, with a rag body added by her mother.

◄ A discarded bedpost inspired this doll made in the 1850s. Her head was carved, then attached to a large cloth body, and she was dressed in lace-trimmed pantalettes and a cotton frock. (Height: 22¼") *Courtesy of the Brooklyn Children's Museum*

Men who were at home with tools they used all their lives lavished their skills on these dolls. They enjoyed making them as much as their children loved playing with them. While fathers whittled, new generations watched and learned: "My ambition," says Paul Engle, "was to whittle as well as my uncle on the farm, who could make a whistle which would really blow, carve little animals out of soft pine, or a tiny rifle with a peep-sight."[3]

One of the earliest wooden dolls with a documented history, "Bangwell Putt," belonged to Clarissa Field, who was born blind in 1765. Her grandfather, Moses Field, a respected trapper and hunter of Northfield, Massachusetts, carved the wooden part of Bangwell's body for her before his death in 1775. When Bangwell was given to the Memorial Museum of Deerfield in 1882 by Clarissa's cousin Deacon Phinehas Field, she was accompanied by Deacon Field's handwritten explanation:

> Clarissa Field, in her girlhood, was very fond of dolls of which s'had several. The following are the names of some of her doll family: Pingo, Palica, Himonarro, Ebby Puttence, Bangwell Putt. This last named was her favorite; and was carefully kept and tended through life. Its body was formed by a jackknife from a piece of pinewood, its hands and fingers were of deerskin, and its shoes were of the same, showing considerable skill in the making. Several dresses had been worn out in tending and replaced by the owner. . . . The wood part was made by her natural grandfather, Moses Field.[4]

Illness and death visited children too often in the eighteenth and nineteenth centuries, causing a preoccupying morbidity that even affected children's toys. "Coffin dolls" first appeared as playthings in the late eighteenth century. These miniature wooden dolls (sometimes clothed) fit inside tiny lidded coffins. Children could remove the dolls from the coffins—to modern minds a rather macabre form of amusement.

Wooden dolls reflecting happier times could be made to dance by strings or by moving a stick inserted in a hole in the doll's back. These articulated dolls were known as "Dancing Dans" and "Jumping Jacks." One of the earliest dancing dolls belonged to William Ellery, of Rhode Island, a signer of the Declaration of Independence. Made from white pine and copper in 1790, it is typical of these popular dolls.

This tiny matchstick doll (ca. 1875) has a painted
wooden head, jointed arms and legs (alas, one leg
is missing), and a cloth torso with a silk skirt.
(Height: 1″) *Photograph by Armen March; courtesy
of the Newark Museum*

Dolls that did not dance but could move and bend by means of pegged or mortised joints called for sophisticated techniques that ultimately led to the patented Joel Ellis doll. However, long before his short-lived commercial venture, many dollmakers made jointed wooden dolls at home. "Erma," a Pennsylvania Dutch doll, stood on a wooden platform equipped with a pedal that, when pressed, caused her arms to fling and her right leg to kick and bend at the same time. Carved, blue-painted doves adorning the platform sides contributed to the charm of this amusing doll.

American dollmakers occasionally copied the popular English "pennywooden" dolls that sold for a few cents in every town and were immortalized by Nathaniel Hawthorne in his novels and tales. Made of crudely carved wood, with movable joints fastened by pegs and faces cursorily painted on, these dolls were sold unclothed. A first cousin of John Wanamaker had such a doll made for her in Philadelphia in 1843 (see page 54), which except for its documented American provenance remains identical to the ubiquitous English versions.

Wooden dolls enjoyed a high survival rate as a result of their sturdy construction. One old wooden doll found in West Virginia had the words "KANT BE BROKE" painted in red across its chest. Other Southern dolls carved in the highlands were called "poppets" by the hardworking, poor mountain people. Their simple dolls, whittled from native woods, are often elderly figures in homespun dresses and work overalls and have lines of hardship etched on their faces.

In the early twentieth century, cottage industries and craft guilds were formed to help rural families supplement their meager incomes. Catalogues sold dolls like the North Carolina couple in their hand-carved chairs (see page 52). These proved so popular that they are still being made today. A Tennessee dollmaker, Helen Bullard, describes the efforts and feelings behind the dolls of Appalachia:

> Deep in the mountains of eastern Kentucky a woman heeds her
> little girl's "keening" for a doll. The child has seen a lovely little
> doll in a store window in the county seat and she longs for one of
> her very own. What to do? There will be no trip to town again
> for months—not until spring. The mother hunts a white piece
> of wood and with her kitchen knife fashions a crude head. She
> digs out two holes for eyes, leaves between them a triangular

mound for a nose, and below it a circular mound for a mouth. With a stub of pencil she marks out the eyebrows and adds dots for the pupils of the eyes. A doll must have hair. The mother goes to her spinning wheel and from the washed wool waiting to be spun chooses a wisp of curly black. Flour-and-water paste fastens it to the top and back of the doll's head. Arms come next, whittled with closed mitten hands from a small piece of wood. Legs need longer and larger pieces. From the ragbag come scraps of flour sack for a body to hold all these pieces together and out back is sawdust for the stuffing. Again the scrap bag is sought; it gives up scraps of printed flour sack for panties and dress. Soon a doll is born and a little mountain girl back-of-beyond has her keening stopped and her arms filled with a new little friend.[5]

Some wooden dolls appear more sculptural than doll-like and reflect many hours of carving. Perhaps they were intended as portraits in wood. Others are anonymous objects made purely for the whittler's pleasure. Some were even conceived as occupational therapy for wounded war veterans. Occasionally, hand-turned lathes speeded up the process of wooden dollmaking. In Nome, Alaska, dolls were hastily turned on the lathe to surprise a group of Eskimo children one Christmas Eve in 1898: "While this young fellow was cutting dolls, another good-hearted lad from California was painting on the faces. He was even considerate enough to make the eyes almond-shaped and the noses flat, just like those of the little boys and girls for whom they were meant."[6]

By the twentieth century, store catalogues brought inexpensive dolls to even the most remote outposts, thereby diminishing the need for homemade wooden dolls. Contemporary wooden dolls are more likely to be created for the carver's own artistic delight and are often regarded as genuine works of art.

This prim, bright-eyed painted wooden doll (ca. 1800) has arms made of pink kid curlers. A white kerchief covers a tuft of real hair. She is dressed in her original linen and lace. Her pantalettes, tied at the knee and reaching to the ankle, were a novelty first seen in the summer of 1806. Her shoes are painted on. (Height: 10″) *Courtesy of and photograph by the Newark Museum*

◄   This proper New Englander might have gone to Yale in the mid-19th c. The hair seems almost brilliantined. The dollmaker took great pains with the joints, so that the doll could assume many positions. The head is delicately carved, while the hands are rather roughly fashioned. (Height: 12½″) *Courtesy of and photograph by the Shelburne Museum, Shelburne, Vt.*

Hand-carved North Carolina dolls of this kind were sold through the Allanstand Cottage Industries, beginning in the 1930s, and proved so popular they are still being made today. This pair—made by Polly Page, of Pleasant Hill, Tennessee—portrays an elderly couple sitting in chairs made of bark. (Height: each, 13½″) *Courtesy of the Brooklyn Children's Museum*

Who would guess that these little figures in their bandannas and aprons are really late 19th c. clothespin ▶ dolls? Their heads are made from burlap and silk, their features painted on, and their tiny wrapped cloth arms attached. Clothespins were among the first American household objects to be turned into dolls, and children are still using them today. (Height: each, 4″) *Courtesy of Bernice Harvin*

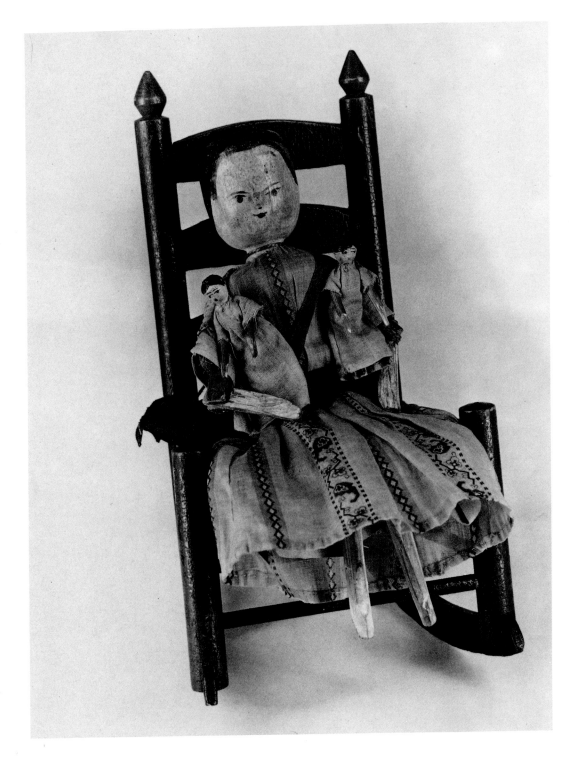

The unusually fine carving of this dancing doll, with its red striped shirt and piercing eyes, brings it into the realm of folk art. Although difficult to date precisely, it was probably made in the late 19th c. (Height: 8½") *Courtesy of Nancy and Gary Stass*

This carved wooden doll, with her painted dress and movable arms, is a true American primitive, a superb example of a type of pioneer doll made in Pennsylvania in the 18th c. She was once in the collection of the sculptor Elie Nadelman. (Height: 9½") *Courtesy of and photograph by the New-York Historical Society*

◄ An American version of the famous English "pennywooden" doll, made in Philadelphia in 1843. (Height: 10") *Courtesy of the Shelburne Museum, Shelburne, Vt.*

Apple, Nut, and Bean Dolls

Apples and nuts from the myriad trees dotting the American landscape inspired imaginative dolls as well as delicious apple and walnut pies. Unlike the corn dolls, which have dual origins in the European and the American Indian cultures, apple and nut dolls were largely indigenous to American soil. As children gathered nuts for their mothers' baking needs, they would save the choicest acorns, pecans, or walnuts for themselves, nibbling a few but saving the rest for dolls.

> More dolls were made of the new young acorns. We'd take a big heavy thread, take the caps off (since they're impossible to sew through), and sew the acorns together in the shape of a long skinny man. These we saved for the Christmas tree, among the first decorations. Later in the winter we'd gild them, so they would shine.[1]

Most nut-head dolls were small, averaging three to ten inches in height, with the type of nut determining the character: "The tilt of her sharp little nose, her pursed mouth, and her keen eyes were not those of a doll. You and I would have known Miss Hickory as the real person she was."[2]

Miss Hickory's pointed face was typical of the hickory-nut dolls, while the smooth surface of the chestnut suggested a more childlike appearance. After a nut was chosen for the head, the body could be fashioned from twigs, pinecones, wood, wrapped cloth or wire, or even pipe cleaners. Sometimes the shell itself was broken into tiny pieces for hands and feet.

◄ This winsome walnut-head couple in their Sunday best appear to be greeting fellow churchgoers. His wife's dress is fashionably adorned with a lace jabot and a brooch. She is clutching a lace handkerchief and a velvet purse. Made of old fabrics, these dolls are difficult to date but are probably early 20th c. (Height: left, 13″; right, 11″) *Author's collection*

Nut-head dolls became an important part of the rich craft heritage of the Southern highlands. Women in the hills of Appalachia found these folksy dolls particularly well suited to express their down-home ways. The women of the Ozarks liked to make their dolls in pairs. "Granma" peered out from under her calico sunbonnet in her best homespun dress while "Granpa" looked on in his faded overalls and work shirt. Some dolls appear all gussied up, as though they were on their way to the Saturday night square dance (see page 60).

In the deep South, nut-head dolls portrayed Blacks in familiar roles. One group at the Newark Museum typifies this very popular type of doll. Made by two elderly Southern women in the 1930s, the dolls carry tiny placards proclaiming "Day Nusry on de Ole Plantation," "Selling Vegetables in Dixie," "A Midnight Visitor," "Uncle Remus," "Farming in Dixie," and "Gettin Ready for Hot Supper" (see page 61). These dolls have colorful cloth bodies, but some nut heads were attached to cornhusk or even tobacco-leaf bodies (see page 67).

The first apple-head dolls in America were made by the Indians, especially by the Northeastern tribes, who used them for "wish dolls." The settlers copied these dolls, and many of the early apple dolls reflected their Indian origins:

> I can remember the first apple dollies I ever saw. They were made
> by my grandmother. . . . The dried apple heads were nailed on
> blocks of wood. Thread was braided and hung down on each side
> for hair. A gay feather protruded from a little beaded band which
> encircled each head. A dark piece of woolen goods wrapped
> around the wooden block completed the blanketed Indian effect.[3]

Traders persuaded the Indians to make apple-head dolls in bright costumes with elaborate ornamentation for the tourists (see page 64). Dollmakers received their inspirations from many sources. Mrs. E. Grannis, of Lewistown, Idaho, saw her first apple-head doll in a Chicago store window and went home to create her own award-winning apple dolls. By 1972, when she reached the age of eighty-five, she had made over a hundred dolls. Miss Isobel Million, of Knoxville, Tennessee, drew from her childhood to create apple-head dolls that reminded her of the mountain people who came down from the hills to trade at her father's store. The peddler "Toby Lemons of Smokey

Cove," and "Rhody Guinn," a weaver of rag carpets and maker of lye soap, were true examples of native American portraiture through the medium of dolls.

Miss Million and other dollmakers chose apple-head dolls to express their feelings because they best suited their artistic needs. The wrinkled faces of apple-head dolls impart character and personality, and are particularly well suited for portraying elderly people. The grandmotherly and schoolmarmish flavor of the dolls on page 63 is enhanced by their wrinkled visages. Even when a dollmaker repeats the same character, she creates unique dolls, since each apple (or prune, apricot, or pear) wrinkles in its own way while drying.

To make an apple head, dollmakers either pinch the features in or carve them while the fruit is still wet. A pointed stick inserted in the head forms the base for the body; in the more elaborate dolls wire armature or pipe cleaners can be used. Because fruit shrinks and darkens as it dries, lemon juice is sometimes applied to retard the darkening agent. Many types of fixatives, including shellac, protect the later dolls.

Apple-head dolls, being naturally great storytellers, are often made in groups as part of scenarios holding special meaning for the dollmaker. Dioramas designed with these dolls have recreated local settings, scenes from American history, and famous plays and tales to the delight of their beholders. An anonymous dollmaker in Maine during the 1920s or 1930s fashioned an apple-head jazz band. One can almost hear the music as the members play their instruments. Nattily dressed in matching hats and costumes, these dolls seem to be enjoying themselves as much as their audience would (see page 66).

For those with nimble fingers and endless patience, tiny seeds and beans were turned into miniature dolls, many of which lived in homemade dollhouses. Since they were more fragile than their nut and fruit cousins, very few survived the rigors of play. Jane Adams recalled how she and other children made dolls out of seeds: "Smaller seeds that we gathered out in the fields or retrieved from melons also made good little men, turned into women by the addition of scraps of material for skirts and scarves glued on."[4] Dollmakers often become so attached to their seed, nut, and apple "people" that they make them honorary members of their families and communities, fashioning clothing and accessories that fit their distinctive personalities. As Jane Coles, of Warren County, Kentucky, confessed, "I can't give my little people away; they're like children."[5]

These early 20th c. walnut-head dolls were fashioned by turning the walnuts lengthwise so the ends would provide tiny noses. After the faces were painted, and cotton beards, eyeglasses, and hair had been added, they were attached to cloth-wrapped wire-armature bodies. (Height: each, approx. 8″) *Courtesy of Aunt Len's Doll and Toy Museum*

Six dolls from a group of ten made by two Southern ladies in 1930 in South Carolina. All have painted walnut heads and bodies of cloth, leather, and wood, with cotton clothing. Each doll is labeled, from "Uncle Remus" on the left to the cook in charge of "Hot Suppa" on the right. (Height: 7″–10½″) *Courtesy of the Newark Museum*

These apple-head dolls form a tidy group of elderly respectable women—grandma, nanny, and school-marm. Their hair is made of lamb's wool. (Height: each, approx. 8″) *Courtesy of the Brooklyn Children's Museum and the author*

◄ A group portrait: three walnut dolls, a chestnut doll, and a hickory-nut doll. The two tall painted walnut dolls (one with twin babies) have whisk-broom bodies beneath their long print dresses (ca. 1920). The chestnut mammy doll (ca. 1910) cradles a white infant. The walnut pincushion doll (front, left; ca. 1890) wears a satin dress and lace shawl. The 19th c. hickory-nut doll wears a matching lace bonnet, shawl, and apron over her black striped linen dress. Her crinoline is made from pages of an old letter sewn together so she can stand. (Height: 8″–13″) *Courtesy of Bernice Harvin, Alice Quinn, and Aunt Len's Doll and Toy Museum*

Dolls belonging to this walnut group made in Georgia during the 1920s and 1930s are easily identified by their looks, style of clothing, and body construction. Known as "Loveleigh dolls," they are typical of cottage industry crafts of that period. (Height: 11″–13″) *Courtesy of and photograph by Harvey Antiques, Evanston, Ill.*

◄ This Seneca man and woman have faces made from dried apples and bodies made of cornhusks. They are 20th c. dolls from New York State, elaborately dressed to appeal to tourists. Note the arm bracelets, the beading, the fur hat, and the buckskin tobacco pouch. (Height: left, 7″; right, 8″) *Courtesy of the Brooklyn Children's Museum*

These musicians were made in Maine—probably in the 1920s or 1930s—by a craftsman who may have used his own gray hair for theirs. The hats are made of cardboard, decorated with floral satin ribbon; the pants are of suiting material. The piano is of balsa wood. (Height: each, approx. 12″) *Courtesy of Shipyard Point Antiques and the author*

An unusually tall nut-head doll wearing a woven straw cape and sun hat, and carrying a bouquet of dried ▶ flowers. In Bermuda, similar dolls were fashioned from coconut and banana leaves. She herself appears to be made of tobacco leaves, indicating a Southern heritage. The Children's Museum in Indianapolis has a doll like her still smelling of tobacco. (Height: 14″) *Courtesy of Leslie Eisenberg Folk Art Gallery and the author*

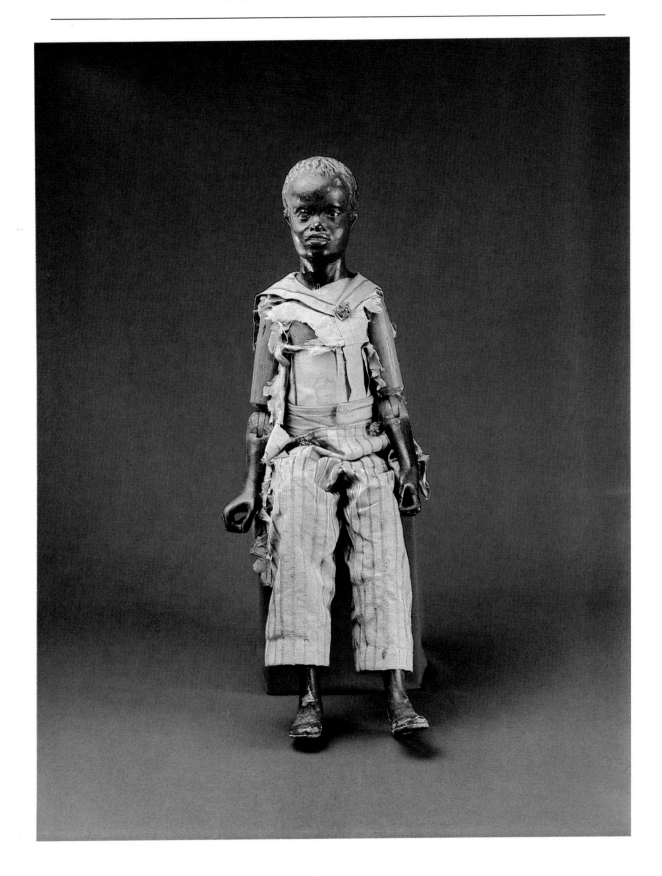

Black Dolls

Black dolls were born in slavery and reflected the troubles of the people they portrayed, revealing a history of prejudice and hardship. Although they were made as playthings, some assuming decidedly comical poses and others created simply to love, most express the poignancy of their place in history. Very little was written about Black dolls; the dolls themselves tell their stories.

The children of slaves played with the cast-off toys of white children or with simple toys they or their parents made. Willa Cather described slave quarters as "littered with old brooms, spades and hoes, and the rag dolls and homemade toy wagons of the Negro children."[1] The plantation, typically self-supporting, contained slaves who toiled in workshops as well as those who labored in the homes and the fields. Slaves who were skilled carpenters, potters, needlewomen, and metalworkers created dolls in their off-hours for the children of their white masters and for their own children. Some of these dolls appeared at Christmas, the one holiday universally observed by even the harshest plantation: "Christmas was approaching. Grandmother brought me materials and I busied myself making some new garments and little playthings for my children. . . . Even slave mothers try to gladden the hearts of their little ones on that occasion."[2]

The few slaves who committed their personal experiences to paper naturally did not dwell on the humble playthings they may or may not have owned. It is mostly through oral histories, often by the children of plantation owners, that we learn of dolls made in the ante-bellum South. One jointed wooden doll carved by an unknown slave on an island off the coast of Georgia belonged to the great-aunt of Marsden Gresham, of Richmond, Virginia. Handed down through the family, the doll is one of the finest and most fully documented slave dolls in America (see page 68). Dressed in his original

◄ A sculpted wooden doll made by an anonymous slave who was clearly a natural artist. Note the elegant rendering of the hands. (Height: 32") *Courtesy of Larry Southworth*

livery of a now-tattered silk shirt with antique buttons, and work overalls, the doll is thirty-two inches high. We cannot know the thoughts of the anonymous creator who carved this masterpiece, but the yearning in the boy's eyes suggests an elusive dream.

Another well-documented mid-nineteenth-century doll had an unusual hand-carved gourd as its head. A slave couple lovingly fashioned this doll (twenty-three inches tall) for their daughter by inserting a stob of wood through a carved hole at the base of the head, which was fastened onto her cloth shoulders by eight tacks. The "gourd doll" is notable for a surviving history as remarkable as its construction:

> The fine, early homestead where this doll was made is still standing on Saluda Street in Chester, South Carolina. Cotton was grown on this plantation. The old home was owned by the Kennedy family. One of the Kennedy girls married into the Coleman family—then from Chester, now from Asheville, North Carolina. The subsequent Coleman children were all born in that home.[3]

Along with rag and wooden dolls, slave children played with crudely cutout tin dolls. Children painted these dolls and dressed them in rags. Only a few of the dolls survived; children threw them on the trash heap when they had outlived their usefulness.

In the plantation nursery, the mammy reigned. To help in raising both the master's children and her own, she conjured up a variety of amusements, including dolls she made in her own image. Some of these dolls cradled Black or white infants in their arms, the tiny dolls swathed in long gowns. The mammies themselves, made from cloth, nuts, or even rubber nipples (see page 81), always wore the traditional bandanna scarf wrapped tightly around the head. Ample figures were almost hidden by the huge aprons that covered simple, homespun dresses. Occasionally one finds a tiny bisque baby (obviously store-bought) that a child had attached to its mammy doll.

After the Civil War, Black dolls gradually assumed the trappings of the middle class and expressed hard-won gains in wealth and social status. They were often made by elderly Black women, and portray ministers, teachers, and fashionable gentlefolk (see page 56). Reminiscent of the Black milliners' models made in Europe, these charming dolls displayed the considerable sewing skills of Black American women. With dressmaking being one of the few opportunities open to Black women, skilled seamstresses vied for the available positions. Then, while they faithfully copied elaborate French gowns for their clients, they raided scrap bags for their children, turning the leftover silks and velvets into elegantly attired dolls (see page 83).

Many dolls known as "character dolls" and "utility dolls" fell victim to racial stereotyping, promoting the image of the carefree, idle "darky" or the faithful servant. Entire families of dolls portrayed life in the rural South (see pages 61 and 80), with the men "goin fishin', poachin', and dancin'." Women nursed broods of "pickaninnies" who were forever eating watermelons. Dolls were incorporated into household objects such as whisk brooms, feather dusters, toaster covers, mops, and doorstops (see page 73). Their upper torsos were stuffed with cloth that covered bottles filled with sand, buckshot, or even old newspapers (see page 82). Occasionally one can spy the date of the newspaper and thereby discover the age of the doll. Many of these dolls were sold by cottage industries to help both Black and white dollmakers supplement meager earnings. In spite of their considerable charm and the skills they embody, these dolls naturally offended many people and fell into disfavor with the rise of the civil rights movement.

Today, both Black and white collectors are interested in these dolls as important artifacts of American history. As a group, they shine with charismatic appeal. The innocence, poignancy, and vitality inherent in Black dolls create a unique tension that transforms these playthings into folk art.

A portrait, shown here in actual size, in pen-and-ink and watercolor made in 1890 by an unknown artist. (3½″ x 4¾″) *Author's collection*

The doll on the left, with button eyes (1930s or 1940s), was made from a stuffed sock attached to a small ▶ feather duster. Beside her is a broom doll, probably made in the 1930s, with hair of steel wool. To the right, a whisk-broom doll made from a silk stocking and dressed in homespun has lost her once embroidered mouth and nose, but kept her earrings and her eyes. She is the oldest doll in the group, probably made around 1910. (Height: 11″–15″) *Courtesy of Bernice Harvin*

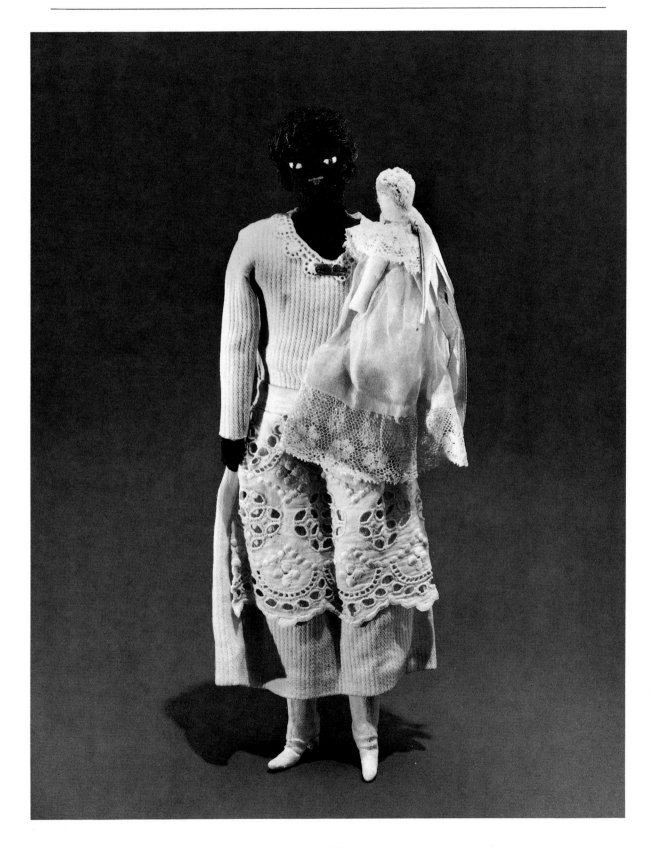

An early cloth gentleman, ca. 1870. His hair is made of mattress stuffing, his eyes of jet beads, and his body of alpaca. His features are embroidered in black, white, and red silk. He is elegant from top to toe, from his bow tie and velveteen jacket to his white-laced velveteen shoes. (Height: 14¾″) *Photograph by Armen March; courtesy of the Newark Museum*

◄ A cloth doll—almost certainly a beloved nanny in a wealthy household—holds an infant in a lace-and-organdy christening gown. Her hairstyle and dress suggest the 1920s. (Height: 8½″) *Courtesy of Bernice Harvin*

A jaunty sailor with an unusual blue velvet face and handsomely embroidered features. (Height: 16½″) *Courtesy of Bernice Harvin*

Two turn-of-the-century dolls, friends meant never to part, their hearts connected by a small chain. ▶ (Height: each, 20″) *Courtesy of Corinne Burke*

A group of rag children, brought together because they look like friends. The earliest doll stands beside the 19th c. painted cradle. Her applied nose, outlined with black thread, gives her a somewhat startling appearance. The other dolls date from the 1930s and 1940s, and the one on the left in the cradle recalls Little Lulu, the popular cartoon figure. (Height: 6″–14″) *Courtesy of Bernice Harvin and the author*

Dolls often appeared in portraits of children, but this watercolor portrait of an early 20th c. mammy doll ▶ by herself is unusual. Though her plaid dress has faded in life, its true color is preserved in her portrait. (Height: 12″) *Courtesy of Bernice Harvin*

Rubber-nipple dolls—here three mammies and a rare male doll—were popular in the 1920s and 1930s and were always Black. Many hold white babies, like the twins in their christening gowns and the little girl held by the distracted-looking doll on the right. (Height: 3″–5″) *Courtesy of Bernice Harvin and Aunt Len's Doll and Toy Museum*

◄ Dolls from the 1930s sold to tourists in the South—part of a group identifiable by their similarly embroidered eyes. The lady holds a bottle of perfume proclaiming "Greetings from Jacksonville, Florida." (Height: left, 8½″; right, 8¾″) *Courtesy of Bernice Harvin*

A touching group of bottle dolls who seem to be posing for a reunion photograph. The mammy dolls, in their bandannas, are dressed in brightly colored prints of the 1920s, while the turn-of-the-century dolls wear subdued linen frocks. The doll second from the left is particularly interesting because of her beaded mouth and because most mammy dolls carried white babies. (Height: 13″–18″) *Courtesy of Bernice Harvin and the author*

These unique dolls transcend their original purpose as "sewing dolls"—dolls glorifying the use of needle and thread—to become splendid works of folk art. They were obviously made by a skilled seamstress who loved her work. They are attached to spools of coarse brown thread labeled "M. Heminway & Sons, Watertown, Conn. Established 1839." They are made of silk, elaborately dressed, their features delicately embroidered. The hair is of wool. The young lady's hat is decorated with ribbons, beads, and sequins; her net blouse is fastened at the collar with a pin, and her skirt tied by a ribbon sash. The tiny beaded sequin sewn to her wrist suggests a diamond bracelet. (Height: each, 8″) *Author's collection*

Indian Dolls

Indian children, like children everywhere, wanted dolls to play with, and their parents responded with miniature replicas of themselves. Since each tribe's mode of dress reflected where they lived and what materials were available to them, Indian dolls are as varied as the tribes themselves. By mirroring a tribe's use of ornament, accessories, and clothing, the dolls accurately record Indian life. For most Indian children, dolls were an integral part of childhood. Beverly Hungry Wolf, a Blackfoot Indian, recalled:

> All that I played with was part of our culture. I had lots of little tepees and all the toy furnishings that go inside. I had lots of dolls also. I was a great one for making dolls. I used wires to start them, then I wrapped the wires to make their bodies, and then I dressed them in Indian clothes. My friends and I made lots of dolls. Those of us who had the longest hair donated some to make hair for our dolls. Then the boys would hunt gophers and squirrels and skin them and we would make the little skins into clothing for the dolls, and rugs for our tepees.[1]

Dolls tell the story of the white man's influence on Indian culture. The first European expeditions to America brought dolls and assorted trinkets for trade with the Indians. In 1585, John White, the artist who recorded the experiences of the English settlers on Roanoke Island, noted that the Indians were "greatlye diligted with puppetts, and babes which were brought oute of England."[2]

◄ A wooden doll found in St. Michael, Alaska, with a papoose just visible in her furry hood. The little half-doll beside her reflects the Alaskan custom of portraying children with a tool or an emblem of adult roles. (Height: left, 13″; right, 4″) *Courtesy of the Museum of the American Indian, Heye Foundation*

By the nineteenth century, Indian women were incorporating ribbons, calico, and stroud cloth into their clothing and dollmaking. Unbending missionary schools exerted pressure on Indian children to learn the language, religion, and customs of the new America. The doll on page 99, wearing the headdress of a nun and the native costume of her people, reveals the dual cultures of many Indian children. Indians in all parts of the country gradually adapted many of the white man's customs, and by the early twentieth century, Indian dolls reflected both identities.

Arctic Dolls

Doll-like figures found in the frozen ground of prehistoric villages testify to ancient Eskimo dollmaking. Early explorers and missionaries believed Arctic dolls to be the first dolls in North America and reported seeing children playing with many different types:

> I suppose there have been dolls among the Eskimos from time immemorial—dolls of stone or bone, scraped and scrubbed into shape with hard flint stones; dolls of wood, with wide-eyed, staring faces, carved after the Eskimo cast with high cheekbones and broad, flat noses; and dolls nondescript, mere bundles of rags, or rather of sealskin scraps, tied with thongs at the waist and neck, and with features visible only to the fond little make-believe mother.[3]

Dolls of bone, antler, stone, ivory, cloth, and skins appeared in great variety and profusion. The carving and polishing of ivory dolls occupied long winter nights and resulted in sculptural dolls of great beauty as well as simple dolls for play. The isolation of Eskimo life contributed to a well-established craft heritage that inspired creative dollmaking.

Survival in the harsh Arctic climate depended upon a well-knit family life, with each member fulfilling his or her prescribed role: the men to hunt and fish, the women to prepare the skins and train the children. Parents gently encouraged their sons and daughters to emulate the roles they would take on as adults. For little girls the mothering of dolls, carrying them about in fur hoods just as their mothers did, occupied an

Resting comfortably on a grass sleeping mat, this tiny ivory-headed couple in sealskin clothing was made in the early part of this century and found in 1925 at Tanunak, Nelson Island, Alaska. (Height: each, 4") *Courtesy of the Museum of the American Indian, Heye Foundation*

The down-turned mouth of the Alaskan ivory-headed doll on the left identifies her as female. The wooden-headed doll to the right has a male face on the side we see, but the head can be turned to show a female face. Note the bushy squirrel's tail that forms the lower torso. (Height: left, 3″; right, 4¾″) *Photograph by Barry McWayne; courtesy of the University of Alaska Museum*

This ivory-headed doll (ca. 1925) has a rag body and sealskin clothing, the rounded face of traditional ▶ Eskimo dolls but the features of a German bisque doll. She is from Tanunak, Nelson Island, Alaska. (Height: 12¼″) *Photograph by Barry McWayne; courtesy of the University of Alaska*

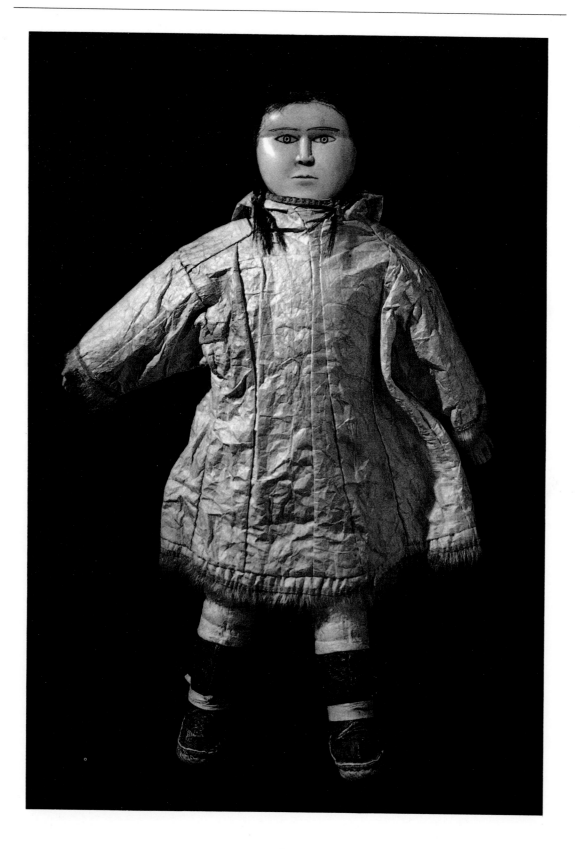

important part of childhood. Even the dolls sometimes carried offspring in their hoods. And some dolls were made with widely spaced legs, enabling them to fit around the necks of their owners. Dolls belonging to little boys were equipped with kayaks and harpoons, heralding the hunters they would become (see page 84). When visitors appeared, Eskimo children acted as proud parents to their dolls:

> While making a brief visit to Sledge Island: two little girls in the house where we stopped amused us by watching their opportunity, while we were busy about other things, to place their dolls standing in a semicircle before us on the floor, while they sat quietly behind as though permitting their dolls to take a look at strangers.[4]

Little girls took care of their dolls, dressed them in the clothes of their region, and made numerous accessories. They fashioned clothing and bedclothes from the skins of mice, lemmings, seals, and squirrels, which they had often trapped themselves. Some of their dolls owned grass sleeping mats (see page 87), baskets, miniature clay oil lamps, and play wooden dishes. In the Bering Strait, little girls stored their ivory dolls in bags of walrus intestines. In Labrador, a doll was more likely to enjoy her own bed: "At night, the child undresses her doll, and lays it to rest on a scrap of reindeer skin spread on a toy bedstead of boards, and covers it with a gay quilt, and leaves it to sleep while she clambers into her own wooden bed and pulls her own reindeer skin or patchwork counterpane over her."[5]

An Ingalik child of eastern Alaska might not be allowed to sleep with her doll because her parents feared evil spirits would enter the doll's body at night. But a persistent child would convince her parents to call the tribal shaman to ward off any lurking evil spirits, thereby letting her have the beloved doll.

In the Arctic, rag dolls were made with muslin, gunnysacking, or flannel. Often lacking facial features, these dolls were simple affairs that grew greasy from children feeding them blubber. Animal skins sometimes replaced cloth dolls, but the "skin dolls" were still stuffed with rags or straw. Even the paws of small animals were pressed into service as hands and feet or as the basic material of the doll (see page 88).

Children's playthings reflected the strict delineation of male-female roles in Arctic life. In addition to including anatomical details, dollmakers sometimes indicated the sex of a doll by the turn of the mouth. An upturned mouth, often with labrets of ivory or beads inserted in the corners, indicated a male doll, while a perpetual frown denoted a female doll. An unusual wooden-headed doll from Tanunak, Nelson Island, possessed two faces—a smiling boy and a frowning girl.

In the lower Yukon, children played with crude dolls of stone and clay. They tucked the arms and legs of their small dolls into scraps of clothing or forgot them altogether. In the Big Lake region (between the Yukon River delta and the mouth of the Kuskok-wim), fathers made unusual bone or wooden swivel-headed dolls. After hollowing out the head and piercing the eyes and mouth through the cavities, they closed the hollow with a thin wooden cover and attached the finished head to the body with wooden pegs. Considering the crude tools available, the construction of these dolls testifies to patient, loving skill. In the Point Barrow region, dollmakers created ingenious mechanical dolls that paddled kayaks, played drums, and danced when pulled by strings. But these wooden dolls were sold to traders and were not widely played with by Eskimo children.

The roles of the trader, the missionary, and the explorer grew in Eskimo life as the frontier pushed northward. Mutual dependency of the Eskimos and the new settlers revealed itself in dolls made as gifts for teachers, traders, and others. A doll might be carved from a single piece of wood with a stovepipe hat, or it might sport a tie. The face of an ivory doll might be made in imitation of a European bisque doll (see page 89). Many of these dolls were played with by missionary children whose toys often reflected a mélange of two cultures. At Christmas, settlers would fashion gifts from the materials found in their new homeland. Evelyn Shore remembered some unexpected gifts in 1920:

> Each package contained a big rag doll. Mine had a deep purple silk dress. It was so pretty that I've forgotten the dresses the other two girl dolls had on. The boys' dolls wore little shirts and overalls. Mother had made the six dolls and dressed them at night, after we were asleep. They were of canvas, stuffed with moose hair, their faces embroidered with colored yarns, and each had yarn hair.[6]

While Eskimo children often played with dolls that wore little or no clothing, the traders requested dolls clad in rich fur parkas or traditional costumes. These later dolls, sporting elaborate clothing and accessories, were directed toward the tourist market rather than to the actual needs of Eskimo children.

Woodlands Dolls

The forest-dwelling Indians of the East and Midwest, the Woodlands Indians, raised corn as the mainstay of their diet. Many of their everyday products, including dolls, were made from cornhusks. Iroquois, Oneida, and Penobscot children played with corn dolls and probably taught their craft to some of the white settlers' children. Woodlands Indian dolls also included those made from wood, apples, rawhide, and cloth, or a combination of materials. The very early dolls were unclothed except for occasional husk garments. Later dolls wore a blend of European and Indian costumes, reflecting their tribal habit and contact with the white settlers.

The Oneidas and Senecas made apple-head dolls with cornhusk bodies personalizing the spirit "Loose Feet." This benevolent spirit granted the wishes of small children. Its doll manifestations, called "happy heads" or "wish dolls," were given to children as symbols of good fortune and were not intended for play.

The Iroquois fashioned cornhusk and wooden dolls with horse or human hair, braided in the typical Iroquois style and held by a cloth band out of which peeked a few feathers. In wooden dolls, the hair was sometimes inserted at the middle of the crown. Some Iroquois dollmakers left their dolls faceless, fearing that a doll with definite features might turn into the person it portrayed. This belief of latent spirits existing in dolls affected many tribes, and some, such as the Kiowas, banned dolls completely. Other tribes, like the Delawares, fashioned dolls for use in religious rites rather than for playthings.

In the Midwest, the women of the Great Lakes tribes incorporated their love of ribbonwork into their dollmaking. When the traders brought brightly colored ribbons to the Micmac, the Sauk and Fox, the Menomini, the Osage, and other tribes, they inspired a new mode of Indian dress. The women of these tribes used French silk ribbons to decorate their clothing with beautiful geometric designs. Their dollmaking also reflected the new styles; tall, dignified ladies and gentlemen, like the Great Lakes couple on page 93, could easily be identified by their unique ribbonwork.

The Chippewa Indians, a Woodlands tribe of the North Dakota and Minnesota region, made buckskin and rag dolls adorned with floral beadwork. Little girls played with

Elaborate ribbon and beadwork characterize these dolls. The couple on the left were found in Oklahoma and could be members of the Osage tribe. They have human hair, and their dress is a mixture of European and Indian styles. The doll on the right is a 19th c. Potawatomi doll, found in Kansas. Note the abundance of silver ornaments, in her dress and hair, reflecting the influence of German silverwork introduced by traders. Her beaded pipe or medicine pouch is tucked into her waistband for safekeeping. The faces of all three are made of buckskin. (Height: 6"–10") *Courtesy of the Museum of the American Indian, Heye Foundation*

Most Seminole dolls were made for tourists. They illustrate the colorful patchwork style that evolved with the popularity of the sewing machine. The red turban denotes a male doll; the woman is wearing the traditional cape. Of course we have the added clue of the mustache! (Height: left, 12½"; right, 13½") *Courtesy of the Museum of the American Indian, Heye Foundation*

simple dolls fashioned by their grandmothers out of cattails, pine needles, and leaves. For older girls, they made elaborate cutout dolls from the bark of the slippery-elm trees. After 1850, when stroud cloth became available, women stuffed rag dolls with dried moss, often endowing them with unusually large faces. When asked about this phenomenon, one Chippewa woman commented, "The faces of the Indians were wider in the old days than now."[7]

Woodlands Indians liked to decorate their clothing and that of their dolls with silver jewelry. At first they hammered silver coins; later, German silver was used to make brooches and earrings, which signified wealth and status. The Potawatomi doll on page 93 proudly wears the trappings of a well-to-do Woodlands lady, including her silver earrings and ceremonial stickpin, her beribboned sash, and her beaded pipe or medicine pouch.

Seminole and Cherokee Dolls

The colorful dolls of the Seminole Indians reflect their unique Southern heritage. Originally a "buckskin" people, the Seminoles soon discarded their heavy buckskin garments in favor of the cooler cotton clothing of the Florida settlers. By the 1870s, the Seminoles were creating their distinctive patchwork clothing with the newly invented sewing machine:

> The dress is made of brightly colored pieces of cloth sewn on a
> sewing machine, a treasured possession of the Seminole women.
> Long, even strips are cut in a variety of colors from lengths of
> material and stitched together in a pattern on the machine. This
> is cut again, sometimes at right angles and sometimes diagonally.
> These strips are again sewed together.[8]

Seminole women were proud of their many-tiered beaded necklaces, collected strand by strand throughout their lives. A little girl received her first strand of beads at the age of one. Each year, more were added until she reached middle age, whereupon she removed a strand every year until there was only one left. Beaded necklaces, black bonnet-like hats, and patchwork dresses identify female dolls, whereas small red hats and patchwork tunics denote the rarer male dolls (see page 94).

Seminole dolls were either carved from wood or composed of fibers from the palmetto tree. Dollmakers wound the brown threadlike fibers over and over again to build the figure's body and head. Seminole children did not play with these dolls, which were primarily made for sale; instead, they amused themselves with "a bundle of rags, a stick with a bit of cloth wrapped about it. . . . "[9]

The Cherokees in the southern Appalachian Mountains patterned their dolls after the mountain people of their region. Cherokee women cast an appreciative eye on the long gowns of the European settlers and fashioned homespun copies for themselves. Their dolls, usually of cloth with embroidered features, were dressed in the same fashion, closely resembling the dolls of the neighboring white children.

Plains Indian Dolls

The Indians who roamed the Plains depended on buffalo and deer meat for survival. Indian women turned animal hides into clothing and other articles of daily life, which they then decorated with beads and quills. They reserved the most elaborate beadwork for ceremonial costumes and sacred objects. Learning the complex beadwork patterns was an important part of an Indian girl's childhood. While pioneer children embroidered samplers and stitched patchwork quilts, Plains Indian girls practiced beadwork on their dolls' clothing: "Her first lesson in applied beadwork was the decoration of her doll's clothing, straight lines, either continuous or interrupted, being the easiest patterns from which she progressed to diagonal patterns and the familiar 'otter-tail pattern.' "[10]

Little girls carried their dolls in toy cradleboards that were miniature beaded replicas of the cradleboards used when they were infants. As Indian children acquired white people's toys, they sometimes stuffed a china doll into their toy cradleboards (see page 99). When the Indian girls grew older, they played with dolls portraying the adult women they would become:

> As soon as she [a Sioux Indian girl] is old enough to play with
> dolls, she plays mother in all seriousness and gravity. She is
> dressed like a miniature woman (and her dolls are clad likewise),
> in garments of doeskin to her ankles, adorned with long fringes,

96

A Blackfoot girl in traditional dress, holding a typical Plains buckskin doll, painted by Winold Reiss in the 1930s. *From* Blackfeet Indians, *by Frank Bird Linderman; photographed at the Museum of the American Indian, Heye Foundation*

embroidered with porcupine quills, and dyed with root dyes in various colors.[11]

Before the traders introduced the large "pony beads" (about the size of a pea), early dolls were unadorned or decorated with quillwork (see page 101). By the 1840s, tiny "seed beads" reached the Plains, and the era of elaborate beadwork commenced. Translucent seed beads appeared in the 1870s, followed by the metallic beads of the 1880s. Often a doll's age can be determined by studying the size and coloring of its beaded decoration. More muted hues characterize the old-style beadwork, while the brighter colors denote later work. In the early dolls, beads were attached with a sinew; in later examples, the beads were sewn on with cotton thread. However, tribal identification through dolls' beadwork proves difficult because the characteristic patterns of each tribe were later necessarily reduced and simplified.

The Sioux Indians, masters of the most intricate beadwork, at times even beaded the bottoms of their dolls' moccasins. The discovery of dolls wearing such moccasins helped to dispel the notion that adult beaded-sole moccasins were reserved for burial rites. Since Indian tradition forbade children's toys to be decorated with signs of death, finding these dolls along with many worn adult moccasins indicated that the moccasins were used in ceremonies and occasionally in daily life. Nancy Rockboy, a Dakota Indian, gave the following explanation to Juanita Kant in an interview about children's dolls:

> Q: Why are these moccasins beaded on the bottoms as well as the tops?
>
> R: Well, they did that in those days, because they are, as I said, children's. They thought so much of them that they even wasted their beads on their soles too, to make them worth much.[12]

From about 1880 until 1910, beaded-sole moccasins were made on Sioux reservations, before the style fell from favor, suggesting that most beaded-sole dolls were fashioned before 1910. During that period, elaborate beadwork became a passion among Plains women, who decorated articles of clothing, household objects, and toys with beads— often, as Nancy Rockboy said, "to make them worth much." Perhaps the creator of the doll on page 101 had that in mind when she covered its face with bright red beads.

This buckskin doll, with a nun's veil and otherwise traditional Indian dress, is a poignant expression of life lived between two cultures. She might have been made by an Indian child for a favorite teacher at a missionary school, or by a kind Sister for a homesick child. (Height: 8") *Courtesy of Nancy and Gary Stass*

A porcelain doll of European origin encased in a Cheyenne toy cradleboard of beaded buckskin, mounted on a wooden frame. The tiny china doll affixed to the top of the cradle is an amulet to bring good fortune and ward off evil spirits. (Total height: 19¼") *Courtesy of and photograph by the Denver Art Museum*

An outstanding group of 19th c. dolls reflecting the Plains culture. The one on the left, with the eagle painted on its chest, was found in South Dakota and portrays a Sioux ghost dancer. The Sioux hunter in the middle, with a bow and arrow, has a quillwork breastplate. The doll on the right, with the beaded face, perhaps celebrates an Apache puberty rite for which boys painted their faces red. Note the tiny metal cones, called tinklers, hanging from his shirt. (Height: left to right, 10¾"; 15½"; 12") *Courtesy of the Museum of the American Indian, Heye Foundation*

◄ A true hunter of the Plains, this 19th c. Comanche doll is only comfortable astride his horse because he was made with his legs in riding position. (Total height: 9½"; rider, 5") *Courtesy of the Museum of the American Indian, Heye Foundation*

While parents sometimes fashioned elaborate dolls, they did not let their children play with them; instead, these dolls were hung in the tepee for show, to remind the children of their rich heritage. The everyday, rough-and-tumble doll was usually a makeshift rag doll. Agnes Yellow Plume and Anne Wolf, two Arapaho Indians, remembered the dolls they created as children:

> The dolls we played with were rag dolls. They were merely little round heads with rags hanging down. When we made one, we tried to get a piece of cloth of black and white print. The black represented the hair; the white the face. These dolls had no arms or legs. They were wrapped in pieces of cloth to make them look as though they wore shawls. We had several of these shawls and used to change them like white children today change the dresses of their dolls. I had four such dolls.[13]

Indian mothers found dolls helpful in teaching their daughters what was expected of them. Among the Jicarilla Apaches, little girls practiced domestic tasks with their dolls.

> The girls are taught to play with little tepees. The older women give them little dolls made of buckskin. . . . The mother lets the little girl help sew the doll's dress the first time. The next time she teaches her how to sew and tells her to do it herself. The mother teaches her how to cook for the dolls too. . . . And she tells her how to feed the dolls, for someday the girl is going to be a mother and have children.[14]

The little girls of various Plains tribes, eager to emulate their mothers, must have felt like Pretty-Shield, a Crow Indian.

> I tried to be like my mother. . . . I carried my doll on my back just as mothers carry their babies; and besides this I had a little tepee [lodge] that I pitched whenever my aunt pitched hers.
>
> Once several of us girls made ourselves a play village with our tiny tepees. Of course our children were dolls, and our horses dogs, and yet we managed to make our village look very real. . . .[15]

Little boys prepared for their roles as hunters with dolls accompanied by horses (see page 100). Sometimes they helped their sisters make dolls, too. Nancy Rockboy reported seeing Dakota boys playing with dolls on the Crow Creek Reservation in South Dakota. She believed many of these dolls were made for show.

> Q: Did they [the older sisters] make ones for little boys, too?
> R: Yes.
> Q: Could they play with them?
> R: No.
> Q: Could they carry them around?
> R: Yes, to show other children.[16]

Other observers of Plains Indians noted that dolls were only played with by girls. Among the Teton Dakota, Owen Dorsey reported, "None but girls can play Shkátapi Chik'ála, 'playing with small things' in which they imitate the actions of women, such as carrying dolls. . . ."[17]

One would conclude that dolls played the same roles in Plains Indian childhood as in most cultures: while primarily the province of little girls, they peripherally entered the boys' domain.

Kachina Dolls

For centuries the Pueblo Indians lived on the high mesas of the Southwest. Desert conditions made water, or the lack of it, the controlling factor in their lives. The Hopi religion, built around the Kachina cult, evolved as a means of inducing supernatural spirits to bless the Hopis with adequate moisture and sufficient crops. To ensure survival in a land with an unusually short growing season, an elaborate religious calendar was created, with complex rites and dances for each season. According to the Hopis, "A Kachina is a supernatural being who is impersonated by a man wearing a mask. . . ."[18] On a more abstract level, "Kachinas are the spirit essence of everything in the real world."[19] In practice, men donning Kachina masks (Kachinas are never women) visit Hopi villages from late December until late July. Their participation in the ceremonial dances guarantees the survival of the Hopi people: "When a Hopi man places a mask

These Kachina dolls were given to children to educate them in the symbols and rites of their religion, and were usually hung from the rafters of a Hopi house. The baby pictured here would be the first doll a child received. The wolf doll was made by Emery Pohuma in 1954. Note the beautifully carved teeth, made of cottonwood. The doll on the far left is a clown doll, and the doll second from the right represents an owl. The tall doll on the right is a Zuni Kachina doll. (Height: 3″–12″) *Courtesy of the Museum of the American Indian, Heye Foundation*

upon his head and wears the appropriate costume and body paint, he believes that he has lost his personal identity and has received the spirit of the Kachina he is supposed to represent."[20]

By virtue of this spirit, or new identity, the Kachina gains the authority to translate and oversee the laws and customs of the Hopi people, thereby becoming an effective agent of social control. Both the Hopi and the neighboring Zuni observe rites directed toward their children: "Once a year there is a dance held in the plaza, for the express purpose of frightening the children and keeping them in good behavior. Characters of horrible appearance participate in the ceremonies, which are explained to be goblins who come to carry off and devour naughty boys and girls."[21]

On a more positive note, the Kachinas issue sweets and toys such as bows and arrows to the boys, and Kachina dolls to the girls. The Kachina dolls, representing over two hundred spirits, are miniature replicas of the costumed and masked dancers (see page 104). They are not given out as toys but rather as treasured, educational objects to help children identify the many forms and symbols of their religion.

Kachina dolls were presented to infants of both sexes as good-luck symbols (see the childlike doll in the foreground of the photograph on page 104), but after babyhood only girls received them. A little girl's first Kachina doll, often attached to a cradleboard, was a simple figure. As she grew older, the Hopi girl would hang the more elaborate dolls from the rafters of her home as a visible reminder of her heritage. So much is written about the symbolism of the Kachina dolls that one wonders whether Hopi girls had any dolls they could play with. After the arrival of the Mormon missionaries in the 1890s, ordinary dolls played a role in Hopi childhood. In *The Book of the Hopi*, Frank Waters reported:

> The first Christian sect to gain a foothold among the Hopis was the Mormons, who had settled near Moencopi. Here they persuaded a man of the Pumpkin Clan named Tuvi and his wife to adopt their religion—the first Hopis to join the Mormon Church. After a visit to Salt Lake City, Tuvi brought back many gifts, including a children's doll, which the Hopis called a *mormonhoya*, the name still used for dolls.[22]

True Kachina dolls are always made from the dried roots of the cottonwood tree. The dollmaker—often a child's relative—searches for a suitable piece of wood, then carefully carves and sands it into a doll-like form. In so doing, he emphasizes the features that are ritually important by means of simplification and abstraction. After priming the porous cottonwood, the dollmaker selects his colors for painting.

Colors represent the six cardinal directions recognized by the Hopi, but can also indicate benevolence or danger. Early dolls were painted with vegetable dyes, mineral paints, and colored clays, which often faded and flaked in time, leaving the older dolls with a weathered appearance. By the 1940s, tempera replaced the old dyes, only to be supplanted in the 1950s by acrylics. Some people prefer the muted tones of the early dolls; others like the vibrant luster of the modern dolls. After painting, the dolls are clothed and fitted with accessories. Details such as the rendering of shells, ruff, and feathers directly bear on a doll's appeal and value.

Until recently Hopi tradition did not permit the signing of dolls and forbade women to make dolls at all. But after World War II these restrictions were gradually relaxed; dolls are now routinely signed and some are made by women. A new emphasis upon "action" poses succeeded the stationary stances of earlier dolls, which had only rudimentary limbs. (See the modern wolf Kachina doll compared to the Hopi clown doll on page 104.) The nude bodies of the earliest Kachina dolls have been replaced by dolls in elaborate costumes.

With an almost bewildering array of dolls to choose from, collectors often try to define their collections by concentrating on one or two of the many subdivisions of Kachina dolls. For the serious collector, there are books entirely devoted to Kachina dolls that identify the many examples and explain their symbolism. All collectors look for good carving, careful painting, accurate accessories, and imaginative, colorful examples. The early dolls are hard to find, existing chiefly in museums and great private collections, but contemporary dolls are available in galleries and museum shops.

Many Zuni dolls are characterized by cylindrical bodies and stylized heads, and are made of pine instead of cottonwood. Often taller and thinner than the Hopi dolls, they possess tiny feet. Their costumes are less elaborate, usually consisting of simply draped cloth brightened by a few strands of beads and a couple of feathers (see page 104). Fewer Zuni Kachina dolls were made, and they are consequently harder to find than the Hopi examples.

The Mohave and Yuma clay dolls (the former at the far left and right, the latter, the two in the middle) were made for play and for tourists. The colorful body painting, the prominence and definition of the breasts, and the lavish beaded necklaces and earrings are characteristic features. In contrast to most Indian dolls, these are childlike in appearance. Note the non-Indian calico skirt of the doll on the right. (Height: 7″–12″) *Courtesy of the Museum of the American Indian, Heye Foundation*

Yuma and Mohave Dolls

Although Indian children in many regions played with rudimentary clay dolls, the Western Yumas and Mohaves developed clay dollmaking into a distinctive art. Drawing on their prehistoric heritage of figurine making, both groups created clay dolls featuring their tribal body painting and hairstyles.

The Yumas lived on the west bank of the Colorado River. During the gold-rush days, white traders persuaded the friendly Yumas to develop their dollmaking into a serious craft. The traders provided the Yumas with cloth and beads, which they incorporated in their dolls. While Yuma dolls wear simple clothing, they display elaborate beaded necklaces and earrings. Body tattooing and painting, practiced by both men and women, often dramatically embellish these dolls (see page 107).

The neighboring Mohave Indians of California made dolls that were almost identical, with a few subtle differences. The more protruding, rounded eyes of the Mohave dolls and their jutting noses distinguish them from the oval eyes and straighter noses of the Yuma dolls. While the Yuma dolls' horsehair wigs were fastened by a cloth band around the forehead, with the hair ends tucked into a depression in the middle of the head, Mohave dolls' wigs were either attached with glue or replaced by painted hair. Collectors have sometimes confused the dolls of the Yumas and the Mohaves because each group often exhibits characteristics of the other.

The primitive modeling of both types, the appealing facial features, and the abundant tousled horsehair of the wigs contribute to the childlike quality of these dolls, rendering them unique in Indian dollmaking.

Northwest Coast Dolls

In the Northwest, Indian children played with dolls of clay, wood, and cloth. Yurok children of the Oregon area made their dolls from the bluish mud found by their streams. They carried the dolls in miniature cradlebaskets, but were careful not to place more than one doll in a basket because of the Yurok superstition about twins. Rag dolls were popular in the Northwest. In 1857, one observer reported: "The girls were very fond of making rag babies and dressing up clamshells like children. One of these girls . . . had a small trunk full of these rag dolls dressed in all sorts of styles, which she used to parade out whenever her friends came to see her."[23]

Among the Klamath Indians in southern Oregon, playing with dolls was an important part of childhood. A girl's mother or grandmother would show her how to make and play with dolls that were fashioned from any available material, including wood, shredded bark, tules, and clay. By braiding shredded bark, a girl could also make a sleeping mat for her doll.

The Tlingit Indians made very simple dolls from pebbles, pounding them into shape with a hammerstone. Klikitat parents shaped dolls from steamed leather and dressed them in fur-trimmed parkas. These dolls often had applied noses and beaded eyes and mouths.

Although the Indians of the Northwest were renowned for their wood carving, they reserved their skill for ceremonial objects. Most of the wooden "dolls" in museum and private collections were used in religious rites—the dolls children actually played with were of the makeshift variety.

. . . And All the Rest

Wishbones, avocado seeds, dried moss, pinecones, and even flowers were gathered by children and adults for dollmaking. Found objects satisfied the need for playthings, even if most of them did not last very long.

In the early pioneer days, parents filled children's Christmas stockings with fried-cake and doughnut dolls. These mouth-watering dolls and their gingerbread counterparts lasted only as long as the children could refrain from eating them, posing unbearable choices. Annie Kimball recalled how she and her friends

> joyously wrapped up their "dollies," sang to them, took them
> visiting, played house with them, and enjoyed them thoroughly
> until other interests claimed their attention. Because food was so
> precious, the ultimate end was inevitable in spite of . . . accu-
> mulations from grimy hands. But there was no grief or regrets
> and the little bereft "mothers" still loved the memories of their
> welcome short-lived [dolls].[1]

Other ephemeral dolls included the fragile eggshell dolls, which were carefully filled with sawdust, cotton, or bits of cloth. Wildflowers from the pioneer garden yielded colorful, fleeting dolls. The hollyhock doll might have lasted only a day, but was re-created thousands of times each summer and inspired a poem by Annie Tanner, who

◄ These dolls—one a clothespin, one a rag doll—reflect the coming of the Chinese to the West to build the railroads. The clothespin doll was made at the turn of the century, when Chinese men still wore the single braid. He has a buckskin face and human hair. His ribbed silk gown, velvet smock, and serene countenance suggest a sage. The rag doll (ca. 1920s) has muslin feet, and tiny buttons fasten the legs to the torso. (Height: left, 7″; right, 10″) *Author's collection*

fondly recalled the hollyhock dolls from her mother's garden:

> *Did you ever make a hollyhock doll*
> *With a green grape pinned on for a head?*
> *They made such beautiful little girls*
> *With their dresses of yellow and red.*[2]

Dolls made from dried moss and prairie grass, while destined to enjoy longer lives than flower dolls, still suffered from their delicate nature (see page 123), for continued handling left them mere semblances of their original shapes. Their simple, sturdier rope cousins fared better, but were noteworthy only for their historical interest. One of the earliest American rope dolls, now residing in the Wenham Museum, Wenham, Massachusetts, is thus described: "The crudest example in the collection is this hank of tow found in a Wenham attic, braided into the semblance of a doll, reminiscent of some hurried mother's remembrances of the braided flax hung on the flax wheel of her grandmother across the water as a talisman."[3]

Sailors used their considerable rope-tying skills to create dolls for their children during the long hours on board ship. While they now and then fashioned a scrimshaw doll, more often they reserved this time-consuming art for wives and girlfriends. In port, sailors were surrounded by children eager to watch them magically turn the thick twists of rope into dolls:

> "Now I'll make you a rope's end doll," continued Sailor Macklin. . . . Drawing a shining knife . . . he cut off two pieces of rope about six inches in length. . . . This rope was as thick as his thumb, and had a tarry smell. . . . He began to loosen one end of one piece with the point of his knife.
>
> "Hair," he said briefly, as with a bit of string from his pocket he tied the loosened strands tightly. Then the second piece of rope was bound across the first. "Arms," he announced. . . .
>
> For a skirt he folded and draped his own red bandanna handkerchief and tied it just under the doll's arms. . . .[4]

Little girls stood by their mothers' spinning wheels waiting for the "hank dolls" garnered from wool off the spinning wheels. These dolls, like the rope dolls, were simple affairs. It required more time to knit or crochet dolls, which were then stuffed in the same manner as rag dolls (see pages 116 and 117). In November of 1892, *Harper's Bazaar* featured detailed instructions for a knitted boy doll. Directions included the reassurance that "this is an absolutely reliable set of directions." By following the long list of instructions, one could make the doll and its costume, including delicate facial features: "Work two eyes and eyebrows with black sewing silk and lips with red. Sew on brown worsted in little curly rings for hair."

After Sunday dinner, children pleaded for the wishbone from the turkey or chicken. While some of the wishbones were broken over secret wishes, others were saved to be made into dolls. A piece of cork served as the head, or melted sealing wax formed the head and feet (see page 121). Wishbone dolls made by adults were likely to be more elaborate, and some dolls were even accompanied by miniature accessories and furniture:

> These calm ladies were always dressed in the height of fashion.
> Hats actually were bought at the milliner's for them. One dainty
> doll has a complete, minute toilet set. Several have small tortoise-
> shell combs. There are tiny bags and purses, the necklaces are
> brilliant. And one little girl has her own box of ivory dominoes.[5]

Wishbone dolls sometimes doubled as penwipers; their voluminous skirts were well suited for the purpose. Often given as gifts, some of these tiny dolls carried cards stating:

> *Once I was a wishbone and grew upon a hen*
> *Now I am a little slave and made to wipe your pen.*

Penwiper dolls were also fashioned from clay pipes, the bowls forming pointed faces with jutting noses. The eyes, mouths, and hair, penciled or inked on the chalk-white faces, endowed these proper ladies with a haughty elegance (see page 118). Pipe dolls needed their skirts for balance or were fitted into spools of thread. Some of these dolls were "sewing dolls," designed to carry the accoutrements of needlework. Their fashionably wide skirts hid pincushions, their aprons sported pockets filled with needles and ribbons, and tiny straps attached additional spools of thread to their shoulders. Although pincushion dolls were introduced in the eighteenth century, *Godey's Lady's Book* popularized them in the mid-1850s with detailed instructions, which carried these dolls into Victorian homes throughout the country.

Another popular medium, unbaked clay, inspired the simple mud dolls of Indian and pioneer children. Hannah Darrah recalled:

> We children . . . enjoyed playing in the clay of the riverbanks.
> We became quite expert in fashioning dishes, dolls, and whole
> herds of animals out of this clay, which we enjoyed quite as much
> as the children of today their squawking mama dolls.[6]

"Uncle Bill Cornelius" (see page 119) typifies the more sophisticated clay-head dolls that were created by serious dollmakers and sometimes sold in cottage industries. Made by Rosa's Character Dolls, in Homer, Louisiana, "Uncle Bill's" legend was pasted to the bottom of his base:

> Uncle Bill Cornelius, born of slave parents on a plantation in Ida
> County, North Carolina, and named for his young master, came
> to Louisiana when only eleven years old—just after "The Surren-
> der." The white folks have given him a hand-out of cast-off
> clothes which will prepare him for the coming months and proves
> his life-long belief, that "the Lord will provide."

People wandering along the beaches of North America found all kinds of objects useful in dollmaking, including shells, coral, seaweed, driftwood, gourds, cork, and fishnet (see page 126). Little girls favored shell dolls, made from the many types of shells that covered the beaches. Elaborate painted ladies, their long pastel dresses created by tiers of shells, carrying umbrellas also fashioned from shells, decorated many a mantel. These shell dolls were sold to tourists as reminders of a holiday visit, with the most amusing dolls coming from the Maine coastal towns. In an 1867 *Godey's Lady's Book*, dolls are shown made from lobster shells, caricaturing Indian chiefs, witches, Scotsmen, fishermen, and other figures.

One could always find an old bottle left on the beach, in the kitchen, or around the yard to make a doll. A bottle filled with sand or buckshot (and covered with a skirt) formed the base and a cloth upper torso was attached, thereby creating a bottle doll. These dolls were so much fun to make that teachers often used them as class projects, reinforcing lessons in measuring and sewing. The finished results perched on classroom windowsills and were proudly given as gifts to parents to be used as doorstops.

After school, many a little girl rushed home to her paper dolls, spending long hours drawing, cutting, and dressing the dolls she so carefully created. In many pioneer homes, paper, like cloth, was treasured, not to be wasted on playthings. The few paper dolls a child owned received special treatment, pressed between the pages of a book or stored in a box. As paper became more obtainable, children needed little encouragement to spend long winter's days creating armies of paper soldiers (see page 125) and families of paper dolls. A pamphlet published in 1857 told of the early, homemade paper dolls in America. "All that I knew about Paper Dolls when I was a little girl was, that sometimes a kind friend would cut from a long narrow strip of paper (usually the edge of a newspaper) folded a great many times, so that all could be cut at once, a row of little men and women. . . ."[7]

Clothing on the early paper dolls did not include tabs. One attached the clothes with tiny drops of sealing wax, taking great care not to press too hard or employ too much wax for fear of tearing the paper. After the 1860s, commercial paper dolls employed tabs and were sometimes copied in homemade versions. Children often sewed the elaborate clothes they made onto cardboard to protect them from accidental damage, for their beautiful outfits were delicate, sometimes built up of tissue paper, lacy valentines, bits of clothing, and cutouts from outdated fashion magazines. Playing with paper dolls was an acceptable amusement for young ladies as well as children, with some outstanding examples created by women of almost marriageable age. Children could earn extra money by selling the paper dolls they made, as a paper-doll booklet of 1856 makes clear:

> There are now a great many Paper Dolls in the country. I have
> seen many, made by the same person. . . . She is a little girl in
> Boston, who I have heard, is paying for her education, by the
> money which she receives from the sale of them. . . . From
> different parts of New-England, and even from New-York, little
> girls have sent to this store for a "lady," or a "girl," or a "boy,"
> or a "family," and have been delighted at receiving, in exchange
> for their shilling or quarter or half-dollar, an envelope containing
> the doll and its pretty wardrobe. . . .[8]

Whether cut from old cards, newspapers, or colored paper, whether inked or painted, paper dolls reflected the styles and social customs of their era. The Brandt family paper dolls of the late 1880s immediately identify their time and place in American life (see page 124). A collection of handmade paper dolls tells of the love bestowed upon them and whispers of dreamy afternoons in bygone days.

"Jack," ca. 1882 (above, left). "To think of old Jack being kept for 74 years, since I was a little girl in Newtonville. Cousin Mill Howe used to come to visit us Beans, from Lowell, in those days . . . he used Jack as a ball to toss. It must have been Mother Bean who kept that doll stuffed in the first place" (Miss Faith E. Wilcox, New York City, April 1956). "Jack" is a knit doll with embroidered features, bead eyes, and black wool ringlets. (Height: 15½") *Courtesy of and photograph by the Shelburne Museum, Shelburne, Vt.*

This late 19th c. New England doll (above, right) was knit with fine steel needles. He has a silk stockinette head and embroidered eyes, an elaborately trimmed jacket, a stiff white collar with a ready-made bow, and beringed fingers. Note the handkerchief in the gentleman's pocket. (Height: 15½") *Courtesy of Nancy and Gary Stass*

◄ These two friends are knitted dolls similar in style to the ones above. They are dressed for an occasion, although the shorter of the two appears less eager to go forth into society. (Height: left, 12"; right, 15") *Courtesy of S. Millhauser and the author*

These clay-pipe dolls, a mid-19th c. phenomenon, are true Victorian delights. The silk dress of the proud lady on the left shows signs of wear. Underneath her skirts, her pipestem backbone fits into a spool of thread, enabling her to stand erect. Next to her is a more fragile pipe doll, with clothes of yellow paper and hair of white cotton. The bespectacled doll, with painted hair, eyebrows, and rosy cheeks, wears a striped silk dress and matching homespun linen apron and bonnet. It is safe to say that these dolls had positions in society to maintain. (Height: each, 8″) *Author's collection*

"Uncle Bill Cornelius" is a character doll made by Mrs. Rose Wilder Blackman, in Homer, Louisiana, ➤ ca. 1940. He has a wire-frame body covered with cotton and wrapped with thread. His original hat is missing, but he still wears his black overcoat, striped wool pants, and brown leather shoes, and carries his walking stick and sack of clothes. Tourist dolls often depicted local characters—in this case, a fellow who had seen better times. (Height: 8½″) *Courtesy of the Brooklyn Children's Museum*

A mysterious pair of 19th c. wishbone dolls, probably made by children. Their simple buckskin capes are sewn together with rose-colored thread; their heads and feet are of sealing wax, and at the back of their heads a fringe of brown thread was inserted into the wax before it hardened, in an attempt to suggest hair. (Height: left, 2″; right, 3″) *Courtesy of Kelter-Malcé and the author*

◄   This Quaker couple, believed to have come from Pennsylvania in the 1830s, is made from dark brown wax and cotton padding. Wisps of light wool hair poke out from beneath their hats. His suit is made of gray wool homespun, her dress of brown taffeta. His silk knee socks and painted applied boots have nearly disappeared. (Height: left, 7½″; right, 6½″) *Courtesy of and photograph by the Shelburne Museum, Shelburne, Vt.*

A wooden doll—a man of the forest—with pinecone arms, dressed in a suit of dried moss with matching hair and beard. Note his ax and woven sandals, and his bark hat. Date unknown. (Height: 10½") *Courtesy of and photograph by the Shelburne Museum, Shelburne, Vt.*

This unusual doll was probably made in New England in the mid-19th c. She has a head of brown glazed pottery, a stuffed linen body, and white kid arms. She is wearing a Quaker dress of gray cambric, a white linen petticoat, and brown kid shoes, and is carrying a proper purse. (Height: 12") *Courtesy of and photograph by the Shelburne Museum, Shelburne, Vt.*

◄ A 20th c. doll whose head and hair are made from bull kelp found on the beaches in California. She is wearing a simple gingham dress with a fancy net cape, and her features are painted on. (Height: 12") *Courtesy of Aunt Len's Doll and Toy Museum*

These paper dolls are part of a set made by a child in mid-19th c. Boston, using watercolor, pencil, and ink. (Height: 2″–4½″) *Photograph by Terry McGinniss; courtesy of the Museum of American Folk Art*

This paper doll (opposite, top), a cherubic little boy, could have stepped from the pages of a classic turn-of-the-century storybook. His father or brother probably went to Harvard, and his clothes reflect the latest style for boys in 1905. (Height: 4″) *Courtesy of Joan Carol Kaltschmidt*

Part of a set of beautifully executed homemade paper dolls (opposite, bottom), originally more than 40 pieces, portraying the Brandt family and staff in the 1880s. Their clothes had to be attached by sealing wax or glue (there are no tabs), but perhaps the children were content simply to place the clothes over the dolls. (Height: adults, 5″; baby, 3″) *Courtesy of Joan Carol Kaltschmidt*

Notes

INTRODUCTION

1. Janet Pagter Johl, *Your Dolls and Mine: A Collector's Handbook* (New York: H. L. Lindquist, 1952), p. 35.
2. Priscilla Lord and Daniel Foley, *The Folk Arts and Crafts of New England* (Radnor, Pennsylvania: Chilton Book Company, 1965), p. 233.
3. Mary J. Grow Hall in *Heart Throbs of the West*, vol. 9, comp. Kate B. Carter (Salt Lake City, Utah: Daughters of Utah Pioneers, 1948), p. 446.
4. W. L. Calver, *The New-York Historical Society Quarterly Bulletin* 4, no. 4 (January 1921):100.
5. Margaret Jensen Smith in *Treasures of Pioneer History*, vol. 5, comp. Kate B. Carter (Salt Lake City, Utah: Daughters of Utah Pioneers, 1956), pp. 188–189.
6. Hannah Dalton in Carter, *Heart Throbs of the West*, 9:399.
7. Rick Steber, *Traces* (Union, Oregon: Bear Wallow Publishing Company, 1980), p. 18.

CLOTH DOLLS

1. Laura Ingalls Wilder, *Little House in the Big Woods* (New York: Harper & Row, 1971), pp. 74–76.
2. Leonore Gale Barette, *Christmas in Oregon Territory in 1853* (Eugene: Privately printed, 1950; in the collection of the New York Public Library), p. 10.
3. Miss Eliza Leslie, *The American Girl's Book, or Occupation for Play Hours* (Boston: Munroe & Francis, 1831), cited in "Some Home-Made Dolls Circa 1831," Clara Holland Fawcett, *Hobbies*, June 1952, p. 51.
4. Ibid., p. 114.
5. Laura Ingalls Wilder, *On the Banks of Plum Creek* (New York: Harper & Row, 1971), p. 236.
6. "Polly and I," *Children's Friend*, June 1868.
7. Lucy Larcom, *A New England Girlhood* (Cambridge, Massachusetts: Riverside Press, 1889), pp. 125–126.
8. Nina Welles, "The Story of Dan Tibbot," *New England Magazine*, December 1903, p. 487.
9. Sally Cordon in Carter, *Heart Throbs of the West*, 9:441.
10. Eliza Hales in Carter, *Heart Throbs of the West*, 9:418.
11. Edith White, "Memories of Pioneer Childhood and Youth in French Corral and North San Juan, Nevada County, California," in *Let Them Speak for Themselves: Women in the American West 1849–1900*, ed. Christiane Fischer (Hamden, Connecticut: Archon Books, 1927), p. 274.
12. Annie Kimball in Carter, *Treasures of Pioneer History*, 5:186–187.
13. Mary Louise Morris, "Dolls of Old Salem," *Hobbies*, July 1971, pp. 46, 50.
14. Ruth Kelley Hayden, *The Time That Was* (Colby, Kansas: Western Plains Heritage Publications No. 2, 1973), p. 165.

15. Quoted in Eleanor St. George, *The Dolls of Yesterday* (New York: Charles Scribner's Sons, 1948), p. 137.

16. Quoted in Johl, *Your Dolls and Mine*, pp. 37–38.

17. M. E. Acker, "Homemade Dolls for the Children," *Harper's Bazaar*, January 1902, p. 72.

18. Larcom, *New England Girlhood*, p. 29.

19. Minnie Brown in Carter, *Heart Throbs of the West*, 9:445.

CORN DOLLS

1. Frank Chouteau Brown, "'The Old House' at Cutchogue, Long Island, New York," *Old Time New England* 31, no. 1 (July 1940):19.

2. Edward L. Dupuy, *Artisans of the Appalachians* (Asheville, North Carolina: Miller Printing Company, 1967), p. 26.

3. Hubert J. Davis, *Christmas in the Mountains* (Murfreesboro, North Carolina: Johnson Publishing Company, 1972), p. 31.

4. Jane Adams, "Corn Husk Dolls," *Occasional Papers in Cultural History* 1, no. 3 (New York: Brooklyn Institute of Arts and Sciences, Children's Museum, 1963):1.

5. Paul Engle, *Prairie Christmas* (New York: Longmans, Green, 1960), p. 5.

6. Dupuy, *Artisans of the Appalachians*, p. 121.

7. Allen H. Eaton, *Handicrafts of the Southern Highlands* (New York: Dover Publications, 1973. Originally published by the Russell Sage Foundation, 1937), pp. 188–190.

8. Mrs. Johnnie Head cited in *The Doll*, Carl Fox (New York: Harry N. Abrams, 1973), p. 339.

WOODEN DOLLS

1. Edith Standforth in *Still More About Dolls*, ed. Janet Pagter Johl (New York: H. L. Lindquist, 1950), p. 49.

2. Deon Smith Seedall in *Treasures of Pioneer History*, vol. 4, comp. Kate B. Carter (Salt Lake City, Utah: Daughters of Utah Pioneers, 1956), p. 202.

3. Engle, *Prairie Christmas*, p. 15.

4. Phinehas Field in a letter written in 1882. Courtesy of Pocumtuck Valley Memorial Association, Deerfield, Massachusetts.

5. Quoted in Iris Sanderson Jones, *Early North American Dollmaking: A Narrative History and Craft Instructions* (San Francisco: 101 Productions, 1976), p. 106.

6. John E. Baur, *Christmas on the American Frontier 1800–1900* (Caldwell, Idaho: Caxton Printers, 1961), p. 288.

APPLE, NUT, AND BEAN DOLLS

1. Adams, "Corn Husk Dolls," p. 2.

2. Carolyn Sherwin Bailey, *Miss Hickory* (New York: Viking Press, 1946), p. 10.

3. Harmony Most, "The Little People," *Hobbies*, June 1950, p. 40.

4. Adams, "Corn Husk Dolls," p. 2.

5. Annie Archbold, *The Traditional Arts and Crafts of Warren County, Kentucky* (Scottsville, Kentucky: Bowling Green-Warren Arts Commission, 1980), p. 10.

BLACK DOLLS

1. Willa Cather, *Sapphira and the Slave Girl* (New York: Alfred A. Knopf, 1940), p. 21.

2. Harriet Brent Jacobs in *Incidents in the Life of a Slave Girl*, ed. L. Maria Child (Boston: Published by the author, 1863), p. 179.

3. Cited by Margaret Mosley, who purchased the doll from the Coleman family, in a letter to the Abby Aldrich Rockefeller Folk Art Center, written October 25, 1978. The doll now resides in the Toy Museum of Atlanta.

INDIAN DOLLS

1. Beverly Hungry Wolf, *The Ways of My Grandmothers* (New York: William Morrow & Co., 1980), p. 56.

2. Theodore De Bry, *America* (Frankfurt, Germany: 1590), cited in Jones, *Early North American Dollmaking*, p. 25.

3. Samuel King Hutton, *By Eskimo Dog-Sled and Kayak* (London: Seeley, Service & Co., 1919), p. 175.

4. Edward W. Nelson, "The Eskimos About Bering Strait," *Eighteenth Annual Report of the Bureau of American Ethnology*, pt. 1 (Washington, D.C.: Smithsonian Institution, 1899), p. 345.

5. Samuel King Hutton, *Among the Eskimos of Labrador* (London: Seeley, Service & Co., 1912), p. 92.

6. Evelyn Berglund Shore, *Born on Snow Shoes* (Boston: Houghton Mifflin, 1954), p. 21.

7. Frances Densmore, "Chippewa Customs," *Bureau of American Ethnology Bulletin* 86 (Washington, D.C.: Smithsonian Institution, 1929), p. 67.

8. Lorene Moore, "Dolls of the North American Indians," *Lore*, Winter 1964, p. 13.

9. Clay Maccauley, "The Seminole Indians of Florida," *U.S. Bureau of Ethnology, Fifth Annual Report* (Washington, D.C.: G.P.O., 1883), p. 506.

10. Densmore, "Chippewa Customs," p. 62.

11. Charles Eastman, *Indian Child Life* (Boston: Little, Brown & Co., 1917), p. 80.

12. Juanita Kant, "Old Style Plains Indian Dolls," *The South Dakota Museum* 2, no. 2 (1975):37.

13. M. Inez Hilger, "Arapaho Child Life and Its Cultural Background," *Bureau of American Ethnology Bulletin* 148 (Washington, D.C.: Smithsonian Institution, 1952), p. 107.

14. Morris E. Opler, *Childhood and Youth in Jicarilla Apache Society* (Los Angeles: Southwest Museum, 1946), p. 40.

15. Frank B. Linderman, *Pretty-Shield: Medicine Woman of the Crows* (Lincoln, Nebraska: University of Nebraska Press, 1972), p. 27.

16. Kant, "Plains Indian Dolls," p. 36.

17. J. Owen Dorsey, "Games of Teton Dakota Children," *American Anthropologist*, no. 4 (1891):329.

18. Harold S. Colton, *Hopi Kachina Dolls* (Albuquerque, New Mexico: University of New Mexico Press, 1949), p. 2.

19. Barton Wright, *Hopi Kachinas: The Complete Guide to Collecting Kachina Dolls* (Flagstaff, Arizona: Northland Press, 1977), p. 2.

20. Colton, *Hopi Kachina Dolls*, p. 4.

21. William Elroy Curtis, *Children of the Sun* (Chicago: Inter-Ocean Publishing Company, 1883), p. 83.

22. Frank Waters, *The Book of the Hopi* (New York: Viking Press, 1963), p. 291.

23. James G. Swan, *The Northwest Coast* (New York: Harper & Brothers, 1857), p. 199.

...AND ALL THE REST

1. Annie Kimball in *Treasures of Pioneer History*, vol. 5, comp. Kate B. Carter (Salt Lake City, Utah: Daughters of Utah Pioneers, 1952), p. 185.

2. Annie A. Tanner, *My Shining Valley* (Provo, Utah: Brigham Young University Press, 1974), p. 23.

3. Adeline P. Cole, comp., *Notes on the Collection of Dolls and Figurines at the Wenham Museum* (Salem, Massachusetts: Wenham Historical Association, 1951), p. 34.

4. Alice Turner Curtis, *A Frontier Girl of Virginia* (Philadelphia: Penn Publishing Company, 1929), pp. 129–130.

5. *Doll Talk* 2, no. 5 (1939):8.

6. Joanna L. Stratton, *Pioneer Women: Voices from the Kansas Frontier* (New York: Simon & Schuster, 1981), p. 149.

7. *Paper Dolls, and How to Make Them* (New York: Anson D. Randolph, 1856), p. 4.

8. Ibid., pp. 5–6.

This doll's body and hair are made of tied, knotted fishnet, and her head is of cork with painted features. Her black and white book is made of felt. California, ca. 1950. (Height: 6″) *Courtesy of the Brooklyn Children's Museum*

Bibliography

Acker, M. E. "Homemade Dolls for Children." *Harper's Bazaar,* January 1902.

Adams, Jane. "Corn Husk Dolls." *Occasional Papers in Cultural History* 1, no. 3. New York: Brooklyn Institute of Arts and Sciences, Children's Museum, 1963.

Archbold, Annie. *The Traditional Arts and Crafts of Warren County, Kentucky.* Scottsville, Kentucky: Bowling Green-Warren Arts Commission, 1980.

Bailey, Carolyn Sherwin. *Miss Hickory.* New York: Viking Press, 1946.

———. *Tops and Whistles.* New York: Viking Press, 1937.

Barette, Leonore Gale. *Christmas in Oregon Territory in 1853.* Eugene: Privately printed, 1950; in the collection of the New York Public Library.

Baur, John E. *Christmas on the American Frontier 1800–1900.* Caldwell, Idaho: Caxton Printers, 1961.

Brant, Sandra, and Cullman, Elissa. *Small Folk: A Celebration of Childhood in America.* New York: E. P. Dutton, 1980.

Brown, Frank Chouteau. " 'The Old House' at Cutchogue, Long Island, New York." *Old Time New England,* July 1940.

Calver, W. L. *The New-York Historical Society Quarterly Bulletin,* January 1921.

Carter, Kate B., comp. *Heart Throbs of the West.* 12 Vols. Salt Lake City, Utah: Daughters of Utah Pioneers, 1940–51.

———. *Treasures of Pioneer History.* 6 Vols. Salt Lake City, Utah: Daughters of Utah Pioneers, 1952–62.

Cather, Willa. *Sapphira and the Slave Girl.* New York: Alfred A. Knopf, 1940.

Christensen, Erwin O. *Early American Wood Carving.* New York: Dover Publications, 1972.

Cleland, Charles F. "Yuma Dolls." *American Indian Art Magazine,* Summer 1980.

Cole, Adeline P., comp. *Notes on the Collection of Dolls and Figurines at the Wenham Museum.* Salem, Massachusetts: Wenham Historical Association, 1951.

Coleman, Dorothy, Elizabeth, and Evelyn. *The Collector's Book of Doll Clothes.* New York: Crown Publishers, 1975.

———. *The Collector's Encyclopedia of Dolls.* New York: Crown Publishers, 1968.

Colton, Harold S. *Hopi Kachina Dolls.* Albuquerque, New Mexico: University of New Mexico Press, 1949.

Curtis, Alice Turner. *A Frontier Girl of Virginia.* Philadelphia: Penn Publishing Company, 1929.

Curtis, William Elroy. *Children of the Sun.* Chicago: Inter-Ocean Publishing Company, 1883.

Davis, Hubert J. *Christmas in the Mountains.* Murfreesboro, North Carolina: Johnson Publishing Company, 1972.

Densmore, Frances. "Chippewa Customs." *Bureau of American Ethnology Bulletin* 86. Washington, D.C.: Smithsonian Institution, 1929.

Doll Talk 2, no. 5, 1939.

Dorsey, J. Owen. "Games of Teton Dakota Children." *American Anthropologist*, no. 4, 1891.

Dupuy, Edward L. *Artisans of the Appalachians*. Asheville, North Carolina: Miller Printing Company, 1967.

Eastman, Charles. *Indian Child Life*. Boston: Little, Brown & Co., 1917.

Eaton, Allen H. *Handicrafts of the Southern Highlands*. New York: Dover Publications, 1973.

Engle, Paul. *Prairie Christmas*. New York: Longmans, Green, 1960.

Erikson, Erik Homburger. "Observations on the Yurok: Childhood and World Image." *American Archaeology and Ethnology Bulletin* 35. Berkeley and Los Angeles: University of California Press, 1943.

Fawcett, Clara Hallard. *Paper Dolls: A Guide to Costume*. New York: H. L. Lindquist, 1951.

————. "Some Home-Made Dolls Circa 1831." *Hobbies*, June 1952.

Fischer, Christiane, ed. *Let Them Speak for Themselves: Women in the American West 1848–1900*. Hamden, Connecticut: Archon Books, 1927.

Fox, Carl. *The Doll*. New York: Harry N. Abrams, 1973.

Grinnell, George Bird. *The Cheyenne Indians*. Vol. 2. New Haven: Yale University Press, 1923.

Hayden, Ruth Kelley. *The Time That Was*. Colby, Kansas: Western Plains Heritage Publications, 1973.

Hilger, M. Inez. "Arapaho Child Life and Its Cultural Background." *Bureau of American Ethnology Bulletin* 148. Washington, D.C.: Smithsonian Institution, 1952.

Hillier, Mary. *Dolls and Dollmakers*. London: Weidenfeld & Nicolson, 1968.

Holz, Loretta. *The How-To Book of International Dolls*. New York: Crown Publishers, 1980.

Hungry Wolf, Beverly. *The Ways of My Grandmothers*. New York: William Morrow & Co., 1980.

Hutton, Samuel King. *By Eskimo Dog-Sled and Kayak*. London: Seeley, Service & Co., 1919.

————. *Among the Eskimos of Labrador*. London: Seeley, Service & Co., 1912.

Jacobs, Harriet Brent. *Incidents in the Life of a Slave Girl*. Edited by L. Maria Child. Boston: Published by the author, 1863.

Johl, Janet Pagter. *The Fascinating Story of Dolls*. New York: H. L. Lindquist, 1941.

————. *More About Dolls*. New York: H. L. Lindquist, 1946.

————. *Still More About Dolls*. New York: H. L. Lindquist, 1950.

————. *Your Dolls and Mine: A Collector's Handbook*. New York: H. L. Lindquist, 1952.

Jones, Iris Sanderson. *Early North American Dollmaking: A Narrative History and Craft Instructions*. San Francisco: 101 Productions, 1976.

Kant, Juanita. "Old Style Plains Indian Dolls." *The South Dakota Museum* 2, no. 2, 1975.

King, Constance Eileen. *The Collector's History of Dolls*. New York: St. Martin's Press, 1977.

Larcom, Lucy. *A New England Girlhood*. Cambridge, Massachusetts: Riverside Press, 1889.

Linderman, Frank B. *Pretty-Shield: Medicine Woman of the Crows*. Lincoln, Nebraska: University of Nebraska Press, 1972.

————. *Blackfeet Indians*. St. Paul: Brown & Bigelow, 1935.

Lord, Priscilla, and Foley, Daniel. *The Folk Arts and Crafts of New England*. Radnor, Pennsylvania: Chilton Book Company, 1965.

Maccauley, Clay. "The Seminole Indians of Florida." *U.S. Bureau of Ethnology, Fifth Annual Report*. Washington, D.C.: G.P.O., 1883.

McClinton, Katherine Morrison. *Antiques of American Childhood*. New York: Clarkson N. Potter, 1970.

Matthews, Mrs. Sallie Reynolds. *Interwoven: A Pioneer Chronicle*. Houston: Anson Jones Press, 1936.

Merrill, Madeline and Richard. *Dolls and Toys at the Essex Institute*. Salem, Massachusetts: Woodland Publishing Company, 1976.

Moore, Lorene. "Dolls of the North American Indians." *Lore*, Winter 1964.

Morris, Mary Louise. "Dolls of Old Salem." *Hobbies*, July 1971.

Most, Harmony. "The Little People." *Hobbies*, June 1950.

Nelson, Edward W. "The Eskimos About Bering Strait." *Eighteenth Annual Report of the Bureau of American Ethnology*. Part 1. Washington, D.C.: Smithsonian Institution, 1899.

Opler, Morris E. *Childhood and Youth in Jicarilla Apache Society*. Los Angeles: Southwest Museum, 1946.

Paper Dolls and How to Make Them. New York: Anson D. Randolph, 1856.

Paxman, Shirley B. *Homespun*. Salt Lake City, Utah: Deseret Book Company, 1976.

Pearsall, Marion. "Klamath Childhood and Education." *Anthropological Records* 9, no. 5. Berkeley and Los Angeles: University of California Press, 1950.

"Polly and I." *Children's Friend*, June 1868.

St. George, Eleanor. *Dolls of Three Centuries*. New York: Charles Scribner's Sons, 1951.

———. *The Dolls of Yesterday*. New York: Charles Scribner's Sons, 1948.

Shore, Evelyn Berglund. *Born on Snowshoes*. Boston: Houghton Mifflin, 1954.

Spencer, Mrs. Clarissa Young. *One Who Was Valiant*. Caldwell, Idaho: Caxton Printers, 1940.

Steber, Rick. *Traces*. Union, Oregon: Bear Wallow Publishing Company, 1980.

Stratton, Joanna L. *Pioneer Women: Voices from the Kansas Frontier*. New York: Simon & Schuster, 1981.

Swan, James G. *The Northwest Coast*. New York: Harper & Brothers, 1857.

Tanner, Annie A. *My Shining Valley*. Provo, Utah: Brigham Young University Press, 1974.

Waters, Frank. *The Book of the Hopi*. New York: Viking Press, 1963.

Welles, Nina. "The Story of Dan Tibbot." *New England Magazine*, December 1903.

White, Gwen. *Dolls of the World*. Newton, Massachusetts: Charles T. Branford Company, 1963.

———. *European and American Dolls*. New York: G. P. Putnam's Sons, 1966.

White, Margaret. "European and American Dolls." *The Museum*, Winter 1955.

Wilder, Laura Ingalls. *Little House in the Big Woods*. New York: Harper & Row, 1971.

———. *On the Banks of Plum Creek*. New York: Harper & Row, 1971.

Wright, Barton. *Hopi Kachinas: The Complete Guide to Collecting Kachina Dolls*. Flagstaff, Arizona: Northland Press, 1977.

A NOTE ABOUT THE AUTHOR

Wendy Lavitt has lectured widely on American folk toys and dolls, and her articles on early American dolls and American antiques have appeared in *Antiques Journal, The Clarion,* and *Spinning Wheel.* She is the guest curator of the exhibit *Children's Children: American Folk Dolls,* to be held at the Museum of American Folk Art, November 1983–February 1984. She lives in New York—where she was born—with her husband and three children, and is co-owner of Made in America, an antiques shop specializing in Americana.

A NOTE ON THE TYPE

This book was set in a modern adaptation of a type designed by the first William Caslon (1692–1766), greatest of English letter founders. The Caslon face, an artistic, easily read type, has enjoyed two centuries of ever-increasing popularity in our own country. It is of interest to note that the first copies of the Declaration of Independence and the first paper currency distributed to the citizens of the newborn nation were printed in this type face.

Composition by Centennial Graphics, Inc.,
Ephrata, Pennsylvania, U.S.A.

Separations, printing, and binding by Dai Nippon
Printing Co. Ltd., Tokyo, Japan.

Design by Dorothy Schmiderer